THE LIFE OF PRAYER
Mind, Body, and Soul

ALLAN HUGH COLE JR.

WESTMINSTER
JOHN KNOX PRESS
LOUISVILLE · KENTUCKY

Scripture quotations from the New Revised Standard Version of the Bible are copyright © 1989 by the Division of Christian Education of the National Council of the Churches of Christ in the U.S.A. and are used by permission.

Book design by Drew Stevens
Cover design by designpointinc.com

First edition
Published by Westminster John Knox Press
Louisville, Kentucky

This book is printed on acid-free paper that meets the
American National Standards Institute Z39.48 standard. ∞

PRINTED IN THE UNITED STATES OF AMERICA
09 10 11 12 13 14 15 16 17 18 — 10 9 8 7 6 5 4 3 2 1

Library of Congress Cataloging-in-Publication Data

Cole, Allan Hugh.
    The life of prayer : mind, body, soul / Allan Hugh Cole, Jr. — 1st ed.
        p. cm.
    Includes bibliographical references.
    ISBN 978-0-664-23069-2 (alk. paper)
    1. Prayer—Christianity. I. Title.
    BV210.3.C64 2009
    248.3'2—dc22

                                                    2008039355

THE LIFE OF PRAYER

Also by Allan Hugh Cole Jr.
from Westminster John Knox Press

Good Mourning: Getting through Your Grief

Losers, Loners, and Rebels: The Spiritual Struggles of Boys
(with Robert C. Dykstra and Donald Capps)

For Tracey, Meredith, and Holly—
Answers to Prayer

CONTENTS

ACKNOWLEDGMENTS

This book involved a good deal of collaboration. My friend, Daniel B. Morehead, MD, and I discussed it on numerous occasions over the course of many months, and his wisdom and insights helped improve what I have written. Dan and I thought that we would write a book on the subject of prayer together. Although our plans changed, I remain grateful that he held a significant place in the writing process for this book and that he therefore has a lasting presence in it.

It continues to be a pleasure to collaborate with Westminster John Knox Press and its talented and dedicated people. I am thankful especially for the opportunity to work with Julie Tonini, Director of Production, and Emily Kiefer, Publicity and Author Relations Associate. Julie's warm spirit, attention to detail, and efficiency are laudable. Emily's ideas and skills for reaching audiences far and wide with authors' works are impressive. I am also grateful for the fine work of Frances Purifoy, whose copyediting helped improve this book.

My wife, Tracey, encouraged me in words and deeds throughout the writing of this book, as she typically does. She and our daughters, Meredith and Holly, bring me delight beyond words and remain an answer to my own prayers. Allan and Jeri Cole, my parents, gave me one of life's greatest treasures when they introduced me to the love of God and the gift of prayer as a child. Their love and support continue to sustain me in innumerable ways.

I have the joy of teaching at Austin Presbyterian Theological Seminary, a school of the church. The students I have the privilege of teaching also teach me on a regular basis. How gratifying to observe their own vocations taking shape, touching many lives, and pointing to God's love for the world in Jesus Christ. Ted Wardlaw and Michael Jinkins, Austin Seminary's president and dean, respectively, provide exceptional leadership and vision, even as they work earnestly in support of faculty, staff, students, excellence in theological education, and the church.

I am also deeply grateful to Jon Berquist, Executive Editor for Biblical Studies at Westminster John Knox Press, not only for his help with this project, which was significant, but also for his ongoing support of my work and of me personally. Jon's friendship, collegiality, generosity, and sense of humor enrich my life.

Chapter 1
WHAT IS PRAYER?

By day the LORD commands his steadfast love,
and at night his song is with me,
a prayer to the God of my life.

Psalm 42:8

People sometimes struggle with prayer. Difficulties with prayer can lead to their feeling perplexed, if not discouraged, about prayer's value and meaning, and it can also lead to an irregular or nonexistent prayer life. Even if they affirm the importance of prayer for the Christian faith and engage to some degree in a practice of praying, they may also feel uncertain, disappointed, or both when it comes to their prayer lives.

Those who struggle with prayer communicate their labors in different ways. They say things such as

"I'm not exactly sure what prayer is. I want to pray. I feel like I should pray. It would probably strengthen my faith and make my life better. But I don't really know what it means to pray. I don't know what it's all about."

"I feel guilty that I don't pray more often, and that I don't pray better. But I don't think I'm good at praying, so I guess I don't do it very much. I make plans to start praying. Sometimes I try it for a few days. Then I always give up. Sometimes I begin to feel scared to try to pray because I don't do it right."

"I don't sense that anything happens when I pray. I'm not sure that anything happens when anyone prays!

But I do still think about praying. I think about it a lot."

"When I see others praying, and I hear how meaningful it is for them, I think to myself, 'I want that too.' But sometimes, even when I'm praying pretty faithfully, I still think I'm missing something because mine's not like theirs.'"

"Does it count as prayer if you pray in the car, or at work, or in bed? Or is it only right when you pray in church? I'm curious. What are the rules?"

"I want to pray, but I don't do it because I've done some pretty awful things that I'm ashamed of. I don't deserve to ask God for anything."

Do any of these of these comments or questions echo what *you* might say about prayer? Are you curious about it? Do you feel that you want to pray, that it's an important thing to do, and that it would enrich your life and faith, but that you don't know what it involves or how to go about it? When you've tried to pray, have you quickly given up because you felt as though you did it incorrectly or too simplistically, or because you thought that praying made no difference? Have you wondered about the benefits of prayer—whether it makes any difference? How about groups of people praying together? Do you ever struggle with how that works, or wonder if it does? Or have you opted not to pray because you feel unworthy or too "sinful"? Do you ever find yourself wanting to follow the biblical wisdom of praying "in the Spirit at all times in every prayer and supplication" (Eph. 6:18), but you doubt that you could do this and question how you would even begin to try? If you answered yes to any of these questions, then keep reading. This book is for you.

This book examines what prayer is and what it does. It considers questions of what motivates prayer, including why you feel the need to pray even when you think that you don't know how to go about it. It also takes a close look at some of the effects of prayer, helping to deepen your awareness and understanding of what happens when you pray. With these concerns for motivations and effects in mind, this book also suggests ways for learning *how* to pray, by yourself and with others, so that prayer becomes a more central part of your life.

WHAT HAPPENS IN PRAYER?

Several things happen when we pray. We offer God praise and gratitude, thanking God for who God is and for what God offers in Christ. We also call on and commune with God, presenting our needs, fears, desires, and questions along with our gratitude, joys, and offers of praise. In doing so, we summon God's presence and care. Furthermore, in prayer we receive from God the effects of faith. These include healing, guidance, sustenance, and a sense of hope, meaning, and purpose in our lives. Most important, prayer encourages faithfulness to God and God's purposes. In prayer we offer devotion to God, responding faithfully to God's grace and claim on us in Christ. Through prayer we also join with God to participate in divine purposes—for ourselves, our neighbors, and the world. Furthermore, Christian understandings of prayer include the belief that praying has an effect on God. Prayer influences how God interacts with the created order, which includes how God interacts with us.

But prayer also has an influence on the one who

prays. The nineteenth-century theologian Søren Kierke-gaard urged that we look mainly not on how prayer changes God but on how it changes us, for herein we find its utmost power and value. As I will point out, prayer can have a significant effect on those who pray. Foremost, prayer helps you become more aware of God, of God's presence in your own life and in the lives of others, and of God's activity in the world. Praying helps you see yourself, others, and the world around you more as Jesus did, so that you, like him, may live more fully aware of God's desires for all of creation. Another way of thinking about it is that as you pray, you become more conformed to Christ and thus to God's will and ways. Prayer thus lies at the heart of living as Christ's people and of living more mean-ingful, faithful, and whole lives. As Christians we all bene-fit from a greater understanding of prayer and from learning how to do it.

THE CHIEF EXERCISE OF FAITH

John Calvin, a sixteenth-century pastor and theologian, recognized the significance of prayer for the Christian life. He called prayer "the chief exercise of faith." This book encourages you to learn more about this "exercise" and to engage in it on a regular basis. "Exercising your faith" actually has two connotations. The first suggests that faith must be carried out or implemented. It must be intention-ally engaged, performed, or put into effect. For faith to make any difference to God or have a bearing on your life, it requires your enactment and effort. You exercise your faith like you exercise the privilege to vote in a free society, exercise the right to free speech, exercise a clause in an employment contract, or exercise stock options that you have been awarded. To pray involves exercising your faith in this sense.

The second connotation of "exercising your faith" suggests efforts to enhance form, fitness, or vitality. In this sense, to exercise faith means to train in it or practice at it, to work out or otherwise prepare for improving your performance as one who follows Jesus. Like the athlete who trains for a sporting event, the pianist who practices for a recital, or the singer who works out her voice to get ready for a concert, the Christian prays in order to live (perform) more vitally (faithfully) in accordance with God's claim and purpose through Christ. This book encourages you to *exercise* your faith in *both* senses of the term. I want you to perform your faith and to enhance its vitality by learning more about prayer and by becoming increasingly dedicated to practicing it.

WHY THIS BOOK?

This book offers an alternative to two approaches to prayer currently in fashion. Let's call the first approach "New Thought" spirituality. It often prefers the practice of "meditation" over prayer, drawing on insights taken from numerous world religions, an eclectic group of philosophies, and various practices relating to both religious and nonreligious interests. While not necessarily harmful or destructive, some of these insights seem foreign to Christianity if not altogether incompatible with its basic beliefs. Examples of popular "New Thought" devotees include Wayne Dyer, Deepak Chopra, and Marianne Williamson.

The other approach takes as its basis what I would

describe as principles for "health and wealth," "success," or what one could call "the gospel of prosperity." It is often employed by popular televangelists, and well-known devotees of this approach include Joel Osteen, Joyce Meyer, Creflo Dollar, and Robert Schuller. Though emphasizing different aspects of Christian faith and life, each espouses prayer and the life of faith itself largely as means for achieving happiness, wealth, professional success, health, and the admiration of other people. In this approach, the principal virtues of prayer follow from its ability to give us what we might most want in life, so long as we pray often enough and do it the correct way.

For many mainstream Christians, both the "New Thought" and "prosperity gospel" approaches leave much to be desired. The alternative approach to prayer suggested in this book has its basis in classical biblical and theological points of view while also drawing insights from psychology. This approach is more suggestive than prescriptive and seeks merely to provide some guideposts for your faith journey. You will discern yourself how best to pray *as* you pray and as you draw from riches in your own faith tradition (if you are part of one). I simply want to encourage you to practice prayer more intentionally, thoughtfully, and regularly, and to suggest ways to do this. I also urge that you consider doing so not merely by yourself but also with others in a praying community, so that prayer becomes for *you* the chief exercise of faith and one that helps you pray for keeps.

A PRAYER FOR YOU TO PRAY

(Prepare yourself to pray by getting yourself still, taking a few breaths, and opening yourself up to God.)

O God, among your greatest gifts is the gift of prayer. You invite us to pray, and we can trust that you will help us do so. I want to learn more about prayer. I also want to learn how to pray. Give me patience, interest, and trust as I seek a more prayerful life. I ask these things in Jesus' name. Amen.

Chapter 2

WHY DO WE PRAY?

I love the LORD, because he has heard
my voice and my supplications.
Because he has inclined his ear to me,
therefore I will call on him as long as I live.
Psalm 116:1–2

I have known some prayerful people. A few have been like "Sarah," a church member and one of those people who just *looked* prayerful. She seemed to approach life as if it were an ongoing prayer to be lived out. Exuding peacefulness, gratitude, gentleness, and hope, hers was a noticeably "God-centered" way of living. Sarah demonstrated a firm commitment to following Jesus with confidence balanced by humility and passion steadied by calm. She also had ways of reminding you of the beauty of life and all of God's creation, and she was quick to note how much you miss out on if you begin to take life for granted. Not only this, but Sarah also appreciated life's mysteries, pointing our how they sometimes challenge one's faith and ability to trust. Observing her usually helped others face challenges of their own.

Sarah also could pray with the best of them. When she said a prayer at a potluck supper, when she opened the Bible study that she led with prayer, or when she visited someone who was in the hospital or homebound, it always had the same effect. No one doubted that God was listening. In truth, it was as if God could be seen standing there with her.

Sarah's life had its own share of difficulties. As a matter of fact, she experienced enormous pain with the loss of

an adult child. Her marriage also had its own series of dis-
appointments. So nothing about Sarah came across as
naive or superficial. Nor did anyone seem to think of her as
"holier than thou" or as one who was entirely "saintly."
Most saw her as a prayerful woman who took her faith seri-
ously and enjoyed a deeply felt connection to God, but also
as one who was rather ordinary in most ways and certainly
down-to-earth. One thing is indisputable: Sarah drew others to herself, and many people wanted what she had in the
way of faith, her special appreciation for life, her depth of
compassion, and surely her capacity for praying.

Some other prayerful people I have known, and
probably *most* of them, have been more like "Nelson."
Nelson struggled with prayer, and he made no bones about
it. Sometimes he would tell you this outright. He'd say
things like "Pastor, I'm trying to pray, and trying really
hard, but it's just not working." Or he'd say something like
"Make sure you pray for me because I'm not doing a good
job of it myself." He was also known to say of himself, "I'm
more of a working Christian than a praying one," which
gave further indication of his difficulty with praying. One
time in a meeting that he was chairing, he opened with a
prayer that went something like this: "Dear God, you have
brought us here to do your work. I'm not sure what to pray
for, and I really don't feel much like praying. I think others
here may feel the same way. But we are here, and we trust
that you are, too. So we pray for your guidance and help.
Amen." For Nelson, rarely did praying come easy.

Despite his noted struggles with prayer, however,
Nelson was thought of by many in the congregation,
including his pastor, as a prayerful man. It's true that he
didn't speak all that eloquently in prayer. He seemed simply to cut to the chase when addressing God. Nor did he

seem to live as peaccfully or gently as some others—such as people like Sarah. Nor would anyone have accused him of routinely looking at life with a "glass half full" perspective. Actually, he could be downright ornery at times and could be a bit of a curmudgeon, and he wasn't afraid to look you in the eye and tell you what was on his mind.

Nevertheless, when in his presence you got the sense that Nelson, like Sarah, lived closely connected to God and had a firm commitment to follow Jesus. He routinely demonstrated God's love and the deep trust that comes with faith, but he did so more in his actions than in his words. And when he wrestled with God, his faith, and the church, which he wasn't afraid to do publicly, never did he seem to waver in his resolve to "stick with God" (as he put it) and to trust that to work out well. Consequently, as was true with Sarah, many who knew Nelson admired him and appreciated what his prayerful life involved.

PEOPLE OF FAITH PRAY . . . DIFFERENTLY

Regardless of whether you identify more with Sarah or with Nelson, their examples are instructive. People of faith pray, but they pray differently and with varying degrees of eloquence and confidence. Some people will pray in a manner that seems natural and more or less effortless, as if God was right there with them. Others will grapple for words to utter, will lack certainty that much happens when they pray, and may give off little in the way of sacred presence. Moreover, with different approaches to prayerful living come different personalities, temperaments, and varied relationships and ways of seeing the world, as was true for Sarah and Nelson. Even so, regardless of how their faith takes shape, those who seek a life tethered to God need to engage in acts of prayer, even when doing so proves challenging.

Perhaps this has always been the case. The Bible recounts the ancient Israelites praying on a regular basis and coveting the endless prayers of one another.[1] Moreover, Jesus practiced prayer himself.[2] He also called on his followers to pray and instructed them in how to do it.[3] We know, too, that after Jesus' death and resurrection his followers continued to pray and placed prayer at the center of their common life.[4] These scriptural accounts indicate that prayer takes individual and communal forms and expressions. We will consider several of these forms and expressions later in the book. Most important, the Bible's attention to prayer suggests that it holds an essential place in the life of faith. People of faith pray.

ESSENTIALNESS OF PRAYER

But *why* is prayer essential? Why do people as seemingly different as Sarah and Nelson need to pray? Furthermore, what makes prayer so significant that Jesus practiced it regularly, commended it to those who followed him, and offered numerous examples to guide us? We find answers to these questions in part by focusing on the role that prayer plays in fostering particular traits and activities connected to a faithful and fulfilling Christian life. To put it in a different way, we understand the significance of prayer as we consider matters of Christian *discipleship*.

In chapter 3, we look at discipleship—that is, following Jesus—with an eye toward several "benefits" of prayer, keeping in mind the psalmist's wisdom that we must never "forget all of [God's] benefits" (Ps. 103:2). But first, in this chapter, we consider discipleship in terms of what *motivates* us to pray *as* people of faith. We ask, What leads us to pray and to seek after prayer's benefits? We explore this question of motivation in terms of what *God* does for *us*. God always takes the lead in the relationship that we enjoy with God. Therefore, any consideration of prayer, including why we do it, begins appropriately with a focus on God and what God does. But then the focus shifts to us and to what we do. This focus also receives our attention in chapter 3, where we not only consider the effects of prayer but also suggest what we may do in *response* to God—how we may live as praying disciples of Jesus. In other words, not only do we consider the benefits of prayer, but we also reflect on how we may act *precisely because* God has acted first to invite us into relationship and offered us these benefits. But let's not get ahead of ourselves. Initially, we need to attend to what motivates us to pray, which always begins with God and God's efforts on our behalf.

I suggest three primary reasons for prayer. First, we pray because *God acts graciously toward us.* Second, we pray because *Jesus prayed and invited his followers to pray.* And finally, we pray because *the Holy Spirit empowers us to pray.* Let us consider each of these reasons, keeping in mind that a prayerful life for any one of us will not be the same as it will be for everyone else.

God Acts Graciously toward Us

Prayer begins with God. We pray first of all because God acts graciously toward us. We can speak of God's grace in a number of different ways: God loves us; God chooses human beings for relationship; God forgives us and reconciles us to God's love; and God makes the faithful promise to abide with us always. We receive these gracious offerings in the person of Jesus Christ and in the work of the Holy Spirit as we encounter them in Scripture and in the traditions of the church. Regardless of how we speak of it, grace issues from God's free choice to love us and include us in God's life. As Calvin says, "The prayers in Scripture especially show how the beginning, continuation, and end of our blessedness come from God alone."[5]

It follows from this offer of divine grace that God remains present and interested in *your* life. Never will you find yourself beyond God's close and immediate care and concern. Karl Barth, perhaps the leading Protestant theologian of the twentieth century, says that the God we meet in Scripture and know in Christ Jesus is "more familiar and real than any other reality" and remains "nearer us than we are to ourselves."[6] This relationship with God continues even when you wonder about God's presence or concern, as Nelson did.

> We live in such close relationship to God that "even the hairs of your head are all counted."
>
> Matthew 10:30

These claims suggest that you have no more intimate relationship than what you enjoy with God in Christ. This relationship serves as the foundation on which to build your life, but this foundation exists only because God has come to us in this Jesus, only because God has freely decided to be our God (God *for us*) and chosen us for relationship. We belong first and foremost to God, fully and completely, and this belonging allows us to pray.

Saying that we belong to God affirms at the same time that God does not belong to us. Let's be honest. We sometimes want God to belong to us. And we can easily begin to act as though God does, even if we know otherwise. Similar to the ancient Israelites, Jesus' earliest followers, and the people living both before and after them, we have a tendency to cast God in our own image. In doing so, we may depict God as an extension of ourselves, our desires, and our needs. This tendency can prove especially true when we feel uncertain, uneasy, or distressed, for these are the times when we look to God most urgently for aid. In these cases, we not only want God at the ready; we also want God to be a certain way, to address particular concerns, and to provide for certain needs—namely, our own or those of persons that we love.

Acting as if God somehow belongs to us can have a direct effect on prayer and faith. For example, it can lead to our viewing God as a commodity that exists primarily to serve us and our self-interests, rather than leading us to serve God and God's interests. Moreover, we can begin treating God as "a cosmic Coke machine," such that we merely need to offer God some sort of payment (i.e., good deeds, the right prayers, acts of kindness, various sacrifices), put in our request, and expect to receive something in return from God immediately.[7]

I have heard this way of thinking about God conveyed by numerous people, in both congregational and other settings. It gets stated in different ways:

"How could God do this to me?"
"I've lived a pretty good life, and I'm a good person; why is this happening?"

"I've been praying to God to help Leo with this problem, and God isn't listening."

"I seek after God, but God isn't there. What am I doing
wrong?"

"God must be punishing me for those terrible things I
did as a young adult. Even though I pray and ask for
forgiveness, my life is still a wreck."

"What must I do to get God to hear me?"

Perhaps you have asked similar questions yourself.
Maybe you are asking them right now. Remember, though,
that praying with any of these working assumptions, or others like them, results in prayer that becomes for the most
part a kind of transaction between us and God. Prayer
becomes a way of offering payment for services rendered.
Praying in this manner can lead us to act as if God operates
under our control. We ask something of God, we live right,
so God is obliged to respond favorably to our request. In
this case, we set the grounds and parameters for the relationship that we share with God.

But such an understanding does not reflect what we
learn in the Bible about God, about our relationship to
God, or about prayer. Nor does such an understanding
reflect the way that prayer, in its most faithful expressions,
has been practiced by the church. It's true that our prayers
affect God and how God acts. Barth declares with confidence that "God is not deaf, but listens; more than that, he
acts. God does not act in the same way whether we pray or
not. Prayer exerts an influence upon God's action, even
upon his existence."[8] We may believe confidently that our
prayers always matter to God and even influence God. But
we must distinguish having an effect on God from having
God under control. We must keep in mind the tendency to

affirm that we belong to God while functioning as if it were the other way around, especially when it comes to prayer.

> I call upon you, for you will answer me, O God;
> incline your ear to me, hear my words.
>
> Psalm 17:6

Because we belong to God, it is God who takes the initiative in the relationship that we share with God. Says Barth, God *addresses* us in Jesus Christ. Recalling the words of the Heidelberg Catechism, a statement of faith embraced by numerous Christian churches, our only comfort, both in life and in death, is that we belong not to ourselves but to God in Jesus Christ, who remains faithful always. This is the meaning of grace. So whether speaking of God's love, of God's choosing us for relationship and offering us forgiveness and reconciliation, or of God's promise to abide with us, we must recognize that God acts on our behalf. God acts for us *before* we can act ourselves. We thus belong to God due to God's free and overflowing love, not due to our own efforts to pursue God, live well as "good persons," or otherwise initiate a relationship with God.[9] God acts for us, on our behalf, precisely because God has *claimed* us. The prophet Jeremiah heard God saying to him, "'Before I formed you in the womb I knew you, and before you were born I consecrated you'" (Jer. 1:5). We enjoy a similar relationship to God. So we pray.

Jesus Prayed and Invited His Followers to Pray

We also pray because Jesus prayed and because he invited his followers to do the same. The Bible reveals that God's people have a responsibility to pray.[10] Praying is not optional when one is following Jesus. The Scriptures also speak of a place for both solitary and communal prayer in the life of faith. We give close consideration to both types of prayer in chapter 4. But note here that Jesus not only met this God-given responsibility to pray; he also practiced each type of prayer. He would withdraw to spend time alone, sometimes in deserted places, in order to pray.[11] He also spent extensive periods (including entire nights) in prayer to God (Luke 6:12), and after public ministries of healing, teaching, and preaching, he would retreat to pray by himself. Furthermore, Jesus pointed to the virtues of praying by oneself when warning against self-interested, public displays of prayer that bring attention to the one who prays rather than to God. Even when others were in close proximity to him, Jesus sometimes prayed in soli-tude.[12] The Scriptures reveal that Jesus valued solitary prayer, practiced it, and advocated that others do so, too.

> "Whenever you pray, go into your room and shut the door and pray to your Father who is in secret; and your Father who sees in secret will reward you."
>
> Matthew 6:6

But Jesus also prayed with other people. The Scriptures tell us that "Jesus took with him Peter and John and James, and went up on the mountain to pray" (Luke 9:28). As he approached his death, Jesus prayed in the presence of these same three men in a place called Gethsemane, asking for God's mercy while trusting in God's provision (Mark 14:32–33). Moreover, after his death, Jesus' earliest disciples imitated his practice and prayed with one another: "All these were constantly devoting themselves to prayer together with certain women, including Mary the mother of Jesus, as well as his brothers" (Acts 1:14), and his followers "devoted themselves to the apostles' teaching and fellowship, to the breaking of bread and the prayers" (Acts 2:42). In the words of the apostle Paul, we learn from Jesus' life and witness that those who desire to follow him should seek to "pray without ceasing" (1 Thess. 5:17).

Jesus' understanding of prayer and his way of practicing it grew out of a long line of Jewish faith tradition. Because Jesus was a Jew, he shared beliefs about God with his ancestors, the ancient Israelites. They clung to a deep belief and trust that God listens to the prayers offered to God and that God responds to them with mercy, graciousness, and love. We learn from the psalmist that God "inclines an ear" to those who call on "the name of the LORD" (Ps. 116). Job's friend Eliphaz assures him in the midst of Job's suffering and need, "'You will pray to him, and he will hear you'" (Job 22:27). Karl Barth articulates well God's promise to hear the prayers of God's people and to respond, and also the bold confidence with which we may reach out to God in prayer. Says Barth, "Thou hast made us promises, thou hast commanded us to pray; and here I am, coming not with pious ideas or because I like to pray (perhaps I do not like to pray), and I say to thee what thou hast commanded me to say, 'Help me in the necessities of my life.' Thou must do so; I am here."[13] Jesus lived with this understanding of God's promises. He believed confidently that God's relationship with God's people called for recurring offers of prayer, whether individually or as a community, and that this relationship entailed implicit trust in the promise of God's faithful responses to these prayers.

It's one thing to believe in this kind of relationship with God. It's another thing to embody it and intentionally live one's life by virtue of it. Jesus did all of these things. As the one in whom "all the fullness of God was pleased to dwell" (Col. 1:19), he personified deep and abiding trust in God. "'The Father and I are one,'" Jesus told his followers (John 10:30), and he *lived* as one with God. Moreover, as many of his ancestors had—Abraham, Isaac, Moses, Hannah, Samuel, David, Elisha, Hezekiah, Manasseh, Ezra, Nehemiah, Job, Jeremiah, Daniel, Jonah, and count-less others[14]—Jesus trusted that God remains present and that God provides. He conveyed this trust to his followers, assuring them that God knew their needs and that God would take care of them.[15] Jesus lived his life with the assumption that God never goes away but rather remains always *for us*. This trust led Jesus to pray, to make the act of praying central in his life, and to commend its practice to others.

Jesus' words and example tell us something else about prayer: it involves serious and sometimes challeng-ing responsibilities. Those who want to follow Jesus must pray not only for themselves and those that they love but also for their enemies and persecutors. Jesus also modeled what he commended to his followers. He prayed for him-self (Luke 22:44; 23:34), and he prayed with and for oth-ers (Mark 14:32; Luke 9:15). He prayed for children when they were routinely devalued by society (Matt. 19:13), and he also prayed for his abusers as he was dying on a cross (Luke 23:34). The Bible and the traditions of the church prize the regular practice of prayer for the faithful life because Jesus did.

"I say to you that listen, Love your enemies, do good to those who hate you, bless those who curse you, pray for those who abuse you. . . . Be merciful, just as your Father is merciful."

Luke 6:27–28, 36; see also Matthew 5:43–46

When we consider Jesus' embrace of prayer, especially in terms of how this motivates us to pray, the pastor and theologian Dietrich Bonhoeffer, who was martyred by the Nazis, reminds us of an essential point to keep in mind. Although prayer can arise from the "natural needs of the human heart," needs that will be discussed further in the next chapter, this does not mean that we should think of prayer as a natural right.[16] Nor, as I have suggested, should we see prayer principally in terms of what we initiate or orchestrate. Nor should we pray as a means to some greater end. Rather, we pray because it brings us into relationship with Jesus and thus with God. We pray because God has acted graciously toward us, addressing us and offering to live in relationship to us in Christ. But we also pray because of *Jesus*.[17] *Jesus* prayed. *Jesus* knew God intimately and said that God will listen. We follow *Jesus*. As Bonhoeffer reminds us, we have no stronger reasons to pray than these.

Several implications for prayer follow.[18] The living Christ mediates our prayers, serving as the "great high priest" and interceding on our behalf before God (Heb. 4:14–16; 6:13–20).[19] The living Christ conforms our wills to his own, and thus to the will of God (John 14:7). The living Christ also invites us to make an appeal (supplication) to God to provide for our needs, just as Jesus invited his earliest followers to do (Matt. 6:5–13, 25–33). Let us consider each of these implications.

Christ Mediates Our Prayers

Sometimes we wonder how God hears our prayers. I recall a young child once asking, "How do our prayers get to God, anyway? He must have really good ears!" But queries about prayer come from adults, too. A middle-aged woman, commenting on her own struggles with praying, once remarked, "What's the point? I can't imagine God hearing all the prayers that must constantly be offered to him, anyway." Many people aren't sure if or how God listens to us.

The New Testament says that God hears our prayers and that God hears them through Christ. In this sense, *Jesus* makes our prayers audible to God. Jesus himself said as much. He assured his followers, "'All things have been handed over to me by my Father; and no one knows the Son except the Father, and no one knows the Father except the Son and anyone to whom the Son chooses to reveal him'" (Matt. 11:27).[20] Christians believe, therefore, that in a mysterious and yet decisive way Jesus reveals God and unites us with God.

As the living Christ, Jesus also brings us into relationship to God. We come to know God through faith in Christ. Our faith results in the one whom Jesus called Father becoming for us a heavenly parent, one with whom we enjoy the kind of relationship that Jesus did. Think of it this way. Our own intimacy with God follows from Jesus' intimacy with God and his choosing to reveal God to us. Moreover, we trust that Jesus' choice stems from his love for us and that God loves us, too, just as God loved Jesus.[21]

We come to God knowing that God already loves us.

Receiving God's love in Christ, we enjoy the privilege of having access to God. As Jesus did, we may approach God *as* those whom God loves. The Protestant Reformers reminded the church that following Jesus involves a unique relationship to God. One aspect of this relationship is that you and I may seek and address God directly. We do not require another person or intermediary, including a priest or pastor, to approach or speak to God for us. Because we have been addressed by God in Christ, all Christians may claim their place in the "priesthood of all believers," as the church reformer Martin Luther reminded us.[22] This priesthood has been granted to us by virtue of Jesus, his faith and fidelity to God, and our trust in him. As Bonhoeffer puts it, "Anyone who is bound to Jesus in discipleship has access to the Father through him."[23] So in prayer we cling to Jesus Christ, who makes our prayers audible to God and who intercedes with God on our behalf.

Christ Brings Our Wills into Conformity with the Will of God

Something life-changing happens as you become bound to Christ in faith and as you cling to him in prayer. Your will becomes more of a reflection of Christ's will, which means that your will reflects more of the will of God. I say more about this in chapter 3 when discussing discipleship. But note here that the Christian life entails living as God would have you live. You live more in sync with the life that God would have for you—indeed you live more in sync with God—when you follow Jesus and hold fast to what God has offered in him. To say it yet another way, following Jesus means imitating him, patterning your life after his life, and seeking to become Christlike. Martin Luther said that living the Christian life involves our becoming "little Christs" for one another. By seeking this status we live more faithfully and authentically as children of God.

Christian life requires us to live as God wants us to live.

In a sense, we look to Christ as the compass for finding our way through life, or in scriptural terms, as the Light that illumines our paths.[24] When following Jesus, we accept that we see most clearly and live most meaningfully and faithfully when we look to him and through him. He reveals God to us. He points to what God desires, how God loves, and what God promises. He also helps us to see others and ourselves as he sees us, and thus as God sees us. This means that we not only look to Jesus to see how to live but also actually seek to see through his eyes, viewing God, the world, other people, and ourselves as he does. We want to adopt his vision, his values, his passion for justice, and his love. We also want to align our wills with his will. When we pray, therefore, we cannot be more faithful than when we ask God to help us become more and more like Jesus.

Jesus Invites Us to Make Our Appeal (Supplication) to God

How can you know whether or not to approach God with your needs? And what may you request in prayer? Many people have these questions, especially when they want to ask something of God themselves. These matters receive fuller attention in chapter 5, where we consider several different types of prayer. But for now, I simply want to emphasize that Jesus told his followers to ask things of God. Not only this, but he also assured them that it is OK to bring their needs to God in prayer, whatever they might be. Furthermore, he provided an approach for doing so, such that the living Christ offers *us* the ability to present God with our own supplications.

In the Sermon on the Mount, perhaps his most influential collection of teachings, Jesus speaks of our relationship to God and of what it means for our lives.[25] He highlights the call of God to orient our lives to God, such that God remains the primary focal point for all that we do. This orientation marks the life of faith. Recognizing this fact, Jesus tells us to pay attention to what we value most in life, saying, "'Store up for yourselves treasures in heaven'" (Matt. 6:20). He urges that we take note of what we seek after in life, what we set our eyes on, saying, "'If your eye is healthy, your whole body will be full of light'" (Matt. 6:22). He also calls us to pay close attention to what or whom we serve, that is, the objects of our deepest passions and highest devotion, saying, "'No one can serve two masters'" (Matt. 6:24). Following Jesus' wisdom, individually and collectively, never ceases to point us to God and to God's benefits.

But notice what else Jesus says. He makes it a point to address experiences of need, and he speaks to how those who have needs may approach God to have them satisfied. Jesus urged that we ask and expect to receive, that we seek and anticipate that we will find, that we approach God and expect God to be there to meet us. God invites us to do so.

> "Knock, and the door will be opened."
> Matthew 7:7–11

Jesus' assurance of God's unfailing presence recalls the words of the prophet Jeremiah concerning God. To the ancient Israelites taken into exile in Babylon by King Nebuchadnezzar, Jeremiah spoke on God's behalf, saying, "When you call upon me and come and pray to me, I will hear you. When you search for me, you will find me; if you seek me with all your heart, I will let you find me, says the LORD" (Jer. 29:13–14). Over and over again, the Scriptures urge "calling upon the name of the Lord," especially in times of need.[26] Jesus urged the same.

Keep in mind that *not* calling on God can mean missing out on what God offers. Not approaching God in prayer resembles a hungry person's passing by a feast that awaits her. A table full of healthy, delicious, and satisfying food has been prepared. But she continues to go hungry because she does not reach out, take what lies before her, and eat.[27] In prayer we reach out to God, calling on God to become known to us. As this happens, we recognize more of God and what God bestows. Moreover, as we pray, we can take note of the sustaining power of God that awaits us, and we can entrust our needs, and indeed our lives, to this power. Says Calvin,

> It is by prayer that we call him to reveal himself as wholly present to us. Hence comes an extraordinary peace and repose to our consciences. For having disclosed to the Lord the necessity that was pressing upon us, we even rest fully in the thought that none of our ills is hid from him who, we are convinced, has both the will and the power to take the best care of us.[28]

Praying to God brings us into deeper relationship with God, which allows us to enjoy God and the "extraordinary peace" that only God provides.

Jesus believed in God's power. As he faced impending death, a time of direst need, he reached out to God in prayer. In a place called Gethsemane, "he threw himself on the ground and prayed that, if it were possible, the hour might pass from him. He said, 'Abba, Father, for you all things are possible; remove this cup from me; yet, not what I want, but what you want'" (Mark 14:35–36).[29] Jesus asked for God to meet his need, and he appealed to God to lighten his burden. He requested that God make his situation different, but as he did so, he also asked that his own orientation to God and to the will of God would endure: "Yet, not what I want, but what you want." Jesus trusted that in reaching out to God he would obtain God's care. This trust buoyed him as he treaded in a sea of danger, distress, and uncertainty. God was there, and God would provide. Like Jesus, we place our trust in God.

The Holy Spirit Empowers Us to Pray

We also pray because the Holy Spirit gives us the ability to pray. Think of prayer in terms of these features: God *invites* prayer; Christ *accompanies* us in prayer; and the Holy Spirit *empowers* us to pray. As concerns the practice of prayer, we pray *to* God, *in the name* of Christ, *through the power* of the Spirit.

The Bible recounts Jesus' promise that the Holy Spirit, sent by God, will teach and provide guidance after his death so that we may continue to live in relationship to God in Christ and to bear witness to Christ in the world.[30] By virtue of the Spirit, which "abides in us," we experience no less than a "new life" (John 14:15–17; Rom. 7:6). We enjoy a life marked by qualities of love, joy, peace, patience, kindness, generosity, faithfulness, gentleness, and self-control

(Gal. 5:22–23). Paul refers to these qualities as "the fruit of the Spirit." The Spirit thus marks our lives in definite ways. It gives us our identities as those belonging to the body of Christ and thereby makes our lives distinctive. In other words, we live differently by virtue of the Spirit working in us and among us, individually and corporately. To put it another way, we live a certain kind of life precisely because we follow Jesus and have been changed by him. As Paul says, we live no longer as ourselves but as those in whom Christ lives (Gal. 2:20). Christ lives in us through the Spirit.

As the conduit of prayer, the Spirit brings about several things in our prayer life. We might think of these as "benefits" for the life of faith. First, the Spirit guides us in how to pray. It helps us with addressing God in prayer so that we know what to say and how to say it. Second, as we pray, the Spirit unites us with others, linking us together in the bonds of faith and friendship. Third, the Spirit gives us strength, perseverance, and peace. We give closer consideration to these latter two benefits that the Spirit provides when looking at the way prayer affects our lives of faith (chapter 3) and the reason praying with others in community remains essential (chapter 4). Here, however, as we conclude our consideration of *why* we pray, let's pay attention the how the Spirit enables and guides prayer.

Many people say that they want to pray with greater consistency and a deeper sense of meaning, but that they don't know how to do this. They state that they would find it easier to pray if they had more confidence in their approach but that they don't know where to begin building their confidence. I remember a person once pointing to this common type of difficulty with prayer when she remarked, "I long to pray, pastor, but I know absolutely nothing about it or where to start." Another person who overheard this remark immediately conveyed a similar concern, stating, "I know what you mean. I get myself ready to pray and the words just don't come. So I sit there feeling silly, like I'm a failure."

We gain the most confidence with prayer by finding ways to practice it in a disciplined fashion, becoming more familiar and comfortable with it, and experiencing God's presence and blessings through it. This familiarity is what I call a "posture of prayer."[31] The more you get yourself in this posture, the more confident in prayer you will become. Later in this book, I suggest concrete ways for cultivating a posture of prayer. In anticipation of these suggestions, however, and as you think about your own experiences with prayer—ones that may include some difficulties with knowing how to pray or where to begin building your confidence—consider more closely the role of the Holy Spirit in your life. In the face of questions or insecurities concerning prayer, you have no better response to offer yourself or others than this: "The Holy Spirit empowers prayer. Jesus made this promise. I require nothing more in order to pray."

> Seeking a "posture of prayer" in all that we do must remain at the center of the Christian life.

The Scriptures provide some help for seeking a posture of prayer. They offer assurance that God gives the Holy Spirit to those who ask in obedience to God, and that prayer invokes the Spirit's presence that fills us and guides us.[32] We could go as far as to say that following Jesus, or living the

Christian life, *assumes* the Spirit's presence and leading. By virtue of following Jesus, we seek to live obediently to God, and we believe that the Spirit makes this possible.

Many people will confirm their awareness of the Spirit's presence. They report living with a palpable sense of God's involvement in their lives. They might indicate this as they note their strong belief in God's "providence," Jesus' "influence" on them, or the Spirit's "guidance" or "direction." They say it in different ways. Some say, "I know that God's hand is in this." Others say, "I can sense the Spirit's leading here." Still others report an approach to life that includes frequently asking themselves the question "What would God want me to do?" Regardless of how they express it, however, these people operate with comforting awareness of God's presence and confidence in God's guiding hand. Sarah was one of these people.

On the other hand, many people who try to live faithfully and who devote themselves to God in Christ Jesus report *not* having such a keen sense of God's presence or evidence of God's working in their lives. This is how it often was for Nelson. Moreover, my experience as a pastor, seminary professor, and church member tells me that scores of faithful people live wondering whether God plays any role in their lives at all. Despite what God has promised would be the case—namely, God's unfailing love, presence, and concern for them—they live with uncertainty about these matters. As a result, when they attempt to pray, they can feel sad, confused, anxious, angry, alone, or as the person previously noted felt, even silly.

If any of these descriptions resemble how you feel, take heart in Jesus' pledge. In his parting words to his followers, he said that the Spirit will remain with us always, even "to the end of the age" (Matt. 28:20). Even when you cannot sense its company, guidance, or concern, the Spirit is near. Even when you have been less faithful, obedient, or interested in God and the Christian life than you'd hope to be, the Spirit is there. So when you struggle with questions or uncertainties, whether about prayer or anything else, you can remind yourself to trust unceasingly in Jesus' words. You can rely on the Spirit's unfailing presence and guidance in your life, when you pray and otherwise. Why? Because God has acted graciously toward you and because Jesus has made you a promise. He said,

> "If you love me, you will keep my commandments. And I will ask the Father; and he will give you another Advocate, to be with you forever. This is the Spirit of truth. . . . You know him because he abides with you, and he will be in you."
>
> John 14:15–17

You can trust that the Spirit remains with you and in you without fail. Jesus has said so. God's love for us always exceeds our love for God. God remains faithful even when we do not.

With regard to knowing what to say in prayer, or how to say it, again you need look no further than to the Scriptures for some help. They tell us not to worry about the inadequacy of our words or the thoughts that inform them. In fact, we discover in the Scriptures that people who consider themselves inarticulate or otherwise inadequate do extraordinary things on God's behalf.[33] So you need not speak eloquently, precisely, or compellingly when you pray, and you do not need to have a pristine life history as a backdrop. Actually, you need not even speak at all. Whether you voice them or not, God knows your thoughts and needs.

God knows them before you know them, and also before you ask God to meet them (Ps. 94:11; Matt. 6:8). You do not pray because God's awareness of your life or what you need depends on it, or because God's interest in providing for you rests on your bringing God into the loop, as it were. Rather, you pray because God has *already* acted graciously toward you, because Christ has invited your prayers, and because the Spirit empowers you to pray.

Furthermore, remember that as you pray you do so accompanied by the Spirit, who actually addresses God on your behalf. The Spirit makes us companions of Christ, who intercedes on our behalf before God. So you never stand alone in prayer. You never have to rely on your own intelligence, your individual gifts for articulate speech, your personal piety, or any of your own devices. Prayer requires simply that you rely on God and what God has offered you. And incidentally, God helps you with this reliance. You need not fret about finding it difficult to pray, for you have ongoing assistance. No less than Christ, through the power of the Spirit, accompanies you.

> The Spirit helps us in our weakness; for we do not know how to pray as we ought, but that very Spirit intercedes with sighs too deep for words . . . [and] the Spirit intercedes for the saints according to the will of God.
>
> Romans 8:26–27; see also Matthew 10:19–20

In affirming that God acts graciously toward us, that Jesus invites us to pray, and that the Holy Spirit empowers us to pray, we not only answer the question "Why do we pray?" but we also confess a deep belief in three claims.

First, God chooses us out of God's love before we can ever choose God. Second, God remains faithful to us in Christ even when we do not remain faithful ourselves. Third, God addresses us before we can hope to address God. These claims have several ramifications for how we may respond to God, including how we pray. We consider these again in chapter 5. Before that, however, we consider further the question of *why* we pray, turning attention to the benefits of prayer.

A PRAYER FOR YOU TO PRAY

(Prepare yourself to pray by getting yourself still, taking a few breaths, and opening yourself up to God.)

> Gracious God, you seek your people out before they ever seek you. I am grateful for your love and your promises made to the world in Jesus Christ. Help me, I pray, to live with greater awareness of your presence and gifts. Help me, also, to share your love with others. I ask these things in Jesus' name. Amen.

Chapter 3

WHAT ARE THE BENEFITS OF PRAYER?

When we pray, our human condition is unveiled to us.
Karl Barth, *Prayer*

As the foundation for the Christian life, prayer tethers us to God in Christ. It also unites us with all people who seek to follow Jesus and to live according to his example. But what identifiable *difference* does prayer make in the lives of those who practice it? What can we expect from a prayerful life, such that if we don't pray, our lives take on noticeably dissimilar forms, expressions, and values? In the next two chapters, we consider these questions by looking at the effects of prayer on those who pray. We pay special attention in this present chapter to how prayer influences, and even shapes, the life of faith—our *discipleship*.

PRAYER AS AN END IN ITSELF

Although we have a deep interest in understanding what happens when we pray, let me stress that prayer remains in essence an end in itself, as opposed to a way to achieve something more significant. Prayer sometimes gets portrayed foremost as an agent for helping to secure something that we desire, such as peace, health, safety, or prosperity. In this case, we pray with at least one eye toward some greater good, which means that although prayer serves as a mechanism for pursuing something valuable, prayer basically lacks value in its own right.

I would liken this way of approaching prayer—that is, as a means to some greater end—to the practice of reading to children in order to help them perform better in school and achieve more success in life. Of course, most parents desire achievement and success for their children. Moreover, we know that reading to children contributes much to their learning, which helps them do well in school and in life. But if one's motivation to read to them stems principally from wanting to help foster their success, then one can overlook much of the beauty, tenderness, joy, and satisfaction that come with the act of reading. One can fail to experience the delight of holding a child in one's lap, being grasped by sticky fingers, catching the scent of just-eaten cookies on the breath or in the hair, teaching and learning from that child, and sharing in the splendor of a young soul's unbridled imagination and excitement. If we read to children while thinking chiefly about how this will help them get ahead in life, then we risk losing out on the matchless blessings of the reading moment.

To view prayer above all as a way toward more significant or valuable purposes involves its own risk, namely, failing to notice and partake in the joy and beauty of the prayerful life. Practicing prayer as a mechanism for getting something, however faithful and appropriate it seems, can lead not only to overlooking the delight that comes with being invited into God's presence but also to operating as if God belongs to us, functions as an extension of us, and exists in large measure to serve our needs and desires.

Operating in any of these ways affects how we view God and our relationship with God. Specifically, we tend to relate to God more for *our* purposes than *God's* purposes.

Checking in with God episodically, when it's advantageous, we otherwise live for the most part without seeking God's presence, guidance, or aid. This leads us to miss out on the joy and satisfaction of living more intimately with God. Moreover, if we sense that our prayers have gone unanswered, which usually involves not getting what we desire, then anger, frustration, and sometimes the loss of hope can follow. At the same time, we invite untold additional burdens into our lives. Why? Because too sharp a focus on ourselves, our needs, and what we must do to get God to help us meet them blurs what God is already doing that nourishes and sustains us. Not noticing God's imprint of grace that presently marks our existence and provides freedom for living less encumbered, we instead take on additional burdens that come with seeing ourselves as ultimately responsible. Whether in prayer or any other aspect of life, we end up carrying an unnecessary emotional, spiritual, and even physical load.

A faithful approach to prayer—like a faithful approach to the Christian life itself—involves recognizing that God has charge over our lives and then relishing the freedom that follows. As a friend has remarked, "Thank God that I don't have to be God." His comment conveys wisdom about prayer. Properly understood, we pray first of all in response to God and out of gratitude to God for what God has *already* done for us in Christ. In prayer we give thanks because we recognize that God has acted graciously toward us, Jesus has invited us to pray, and the Holy Spirit has empowered us to pray. To put it another way, we pray in response to God's being God, faithfully and unceasingly, even as we also recall the wisdom of getting out of God's way and yielding to God's leading. The primary end of prayer is *not* to take the initiative in our relationship to God nor to clue God in to what we need so that we may convince God to provide it. Rather, we pray simply to offer a faithful response to the grace-filled initiative that God has already taken on our behalf and that God promises will endure.

God is in charge—before we pray, when we pray, and after we pray.

Our prayerful response, however, does not end there. We have a further role to play. As the prophet Jeremiah declared on God's behalf, "You shall be my people, and I will be your God" (Jer. 30:22). Leaving God in charge does not suggest that we become complacent or resigned to do nothing, whether on our own behalf or God's. Any true relationship requires mutuality, such that all parties involved contribute in particular ways to forming and maintaining the relationship. It matters in our relationship with God, therefore, how we respond to God's initiative. God will be God. But we must be God's people by responding to God's lead in ways that mirror the example that Jesus gave us.

One such response to God involves prayer. Let us consider prayer in terms of its effects, and, more specifically, how it promotes other qualities and activities desired for the Christian life. In other words, let's think about how prayer helps us live more closely to Jesus' example. Jesus invites prayer precisely because it has a bearing on our lives. Praying makes a difference. Jesus' own words and actions indicate that prayer holds great value for the one who prays. We deepen our awareness of its value and further appropriate the gift of prayer in our lives as we pay attention to what happens when we pray. Taking a cue from the psalmist, we can think about what happens in prayer by noting how it delivers God's "benefits" (Ps. 103:2).

BENEFITS OF PRAYER

As the chief exercise of faith, prayer offers a whole host of benefits to those who practice it. Prayer benefits one spiritually, emotionally, relationally, physically, and in most any other aspect of life that one can imagine. A single book cannot identify, and much less comment on, every benefit found in a prayerful life. Recall the biblical image that portrays the vast number of works that Jesus performed during his life: "If every one of them were written down, I suppose that the world itself could not contain the books that would be written" (John 21:25). We could say something similar about the benefits of prayer.

> Prayer has many benefits!

We can identify several tangible benefits of prayer that call for closer consideration. These benefits include intimacy with God, solidarity with God and others, and faithfulness to Jesus' example. Let us consider each of these benefits, and several related ones, keeping in mind their relationship to one another and to the life of discipleship.

Benefit—Intimacy with God

Any significant relationship requires certain qualities to thrive. These include our attention, time, effort, interest, and commitment. Relationships have a tendency to flourish to the extent that these qualities remain present and garner concern. I'll bet that if you consider your own flourishing relationships, it will be difficult and probably impossible to identify one that lacks these qualities. The same is true in our relationship to God. In drawing one's gaze to God, prayer helps to foster with God these necessary qualities of any meaningful relationship. Through prayer, we attempt to bracket out or discard whatever would turn our attention, time, effort, interest, or commitment away from God, so that our focus on God becomes intentional, immediate, and sharp.

Several years ago, my friend Leslie revealed that she "craved" a better understanding of God and a greater sense of God's operating in her life. She stated, "I am so deeply interested in a stronger relationship with God, but I don't know how to do it. I always sense that God is far away, if I sense anything of God at all." When asked what she thought might help to satisfy her craving, she mentioned several things: reading the Bible, spending more time with people from the church, attending an adult education class focused on how to deepen one's spiritual life, and taking part in worship on a more regular basis. She recognized the value of each of these practices for the life of faith. All of these likely *would* help her strengthen her relationship with God, which she craved.

But it's telling that not once did Leslie mention prayer and how it might lead her to what she wanted. Perhaps she considered prayer that takes place in the context of worship or Bible study, though she didn't mention it, but she never indicated thinking about engaging in prayer outside of these settings or on a more sustained basis. Leslie is not alone. My experience has been that many people who crave deeper connections to God and who long for a more spiritually rich life, like Leslie, can quickly gloss over the value of prayer if they recognize it at all. Truth be told, I have overlooked what prayer has to offer myself. Rarely does my own prayer life get sustained without my conscious, intentional effort. Yet prayer draws us to God and draws God to us like nothing else. No facet of Christian faith or life draws us into an encounter with God as immediately or decisively as prayer. We see this in Jesus' life. Moreover, those who pray testify to the difference it makes in *their* lives. We take no closer look at God or at Jesus than through prayerful eyes.

The attention, time, effort, interest, and commitment that we give to God in prayer leads to greater intimacy with God. Intimacy connotes images of closeness, familiarity, personal knowledge and experience, deep understanding, and significant affection for another. We can expect these qualities to inform any intimate relationship. But intimacy with another human being differs from intimacy with God. When pondering what an intimate relationship with God entails, we should be careful not to assume that we know God fully, or that we may enjoy the same familiarity with God that we do with a spouse, partner, parent, child, sibling, or close friend. God remains in a real sense "wholly other," such that we never know God fully nor recognize God entirely. As Barth pointed out over and over again, God remains hidden from us even as God is revealed to us. Therefore, let's not think of intimacy with God as being marked by complete knowledge or familiarity. Furthermore, our relationship to God never prevents God's freedom outside of this relationship.

"A relation of covenant fellowship requires otherness as well as intimacy, and God never ceases to stand over against creatures as a specific person."

Joseph L. Mangina, *Karl Barth: Theologian of Christian Witness* (Louisville, KY: Westminster John Knox Press, 2004), 60.

At the same time, the Scriptures tell us that God remains near to us, so close that God hears when we call (Ps. 34:18; 145:18). Read as a whole, the entire biblical story conveys God's desire to be God for all people, to know them intimately, and to remain present in their lives. We see this desire most clearly manifested in the life, death, and resurrection of Jesus. As Barth suggests, "God looks at Christ, and it is through him that he looks at us."[1] Our intimacy with God thus remains inseparable from Christ. Moreover, this intimacy deepens by virtue of Christ and the closeness that we enjoy with him. Faith in Christ results in the one whom Jesus called "Father" becoming for us a heavenly parent. Like Jesus, we trust God, rely on God, learn from God, and allow God to guide us throughout our lives.

Prayer fosters this kind of intimacy by bringing into sharper focus the view that we get of God's nature, purposes, and provision through Christ. As a result, prayer leads to greater knowledge of God and familiarity with God. Such knowledge and familiarity prompt us continuously to clarify our relationship to God, deepen our awareness of God's claim on us, and recognize and fulfill our responsibilities to live as God desires. Just as we tend to know other people best by virtue of spending time with them, paying close attention to them, and committing ourselves to them, we become better acquainted with God through prayerful acts that keep pointing us to Jesus and his witness.

Although intimacy with God fosters knowledge of God and awareness of God's hand in our lives, this intimacy also deepens *self-knowledge*. We must not forget this. Like St. Augustine, Calvin observed that we cannot separate knowledge of God and self-knowledge. We do not know God without knowing ourselves; and we cannot know ourselves without knowing God.[2] In promoting greater intimacy with God, prayer helps cultivate both types of knowledge. Prayer does so by calling our attention to God, to ourselves, and to the relationship that we share. At the same time, prayer strengthens this very relationship. The belief that human beings have been created in God's image, which classical Christianity affirms, lends further importance to recognizing the intrinsic relationship between knowing God and knowing oneself.

This intimacy with God that leads to greater knowledge of God and of oneself can lead to several related benefits. One is a deepening capacity for discernment. The more we learn about God and ourselves, the greater our ability to perceive God's presence, to discern what we need, to notice God's hand in our lives, to distinguish God's purposes from our own, and to make judgments about the innumerable life choices that come our way. The more we know, the more discerning we can be.

Another benefit is to deepen our capacity for trusting God—our faith. With intimacy comes confidence in the one with whom we are intimate. As we become more aware of God's presence and provision, relying on both more fully and routinely, we develop a pervasive faith in who God is and what God has promised on our behalf.

With faith comes even greater reliance, which itself produces deeper faith.

One additional benefit, the capacity for gratitude, also relates to greater intimacy with God. As we draw closer to God in prayer, we live with deeper thanksgiving to God. Why? Because prayer helps us to recognize more clearly who God is, what God provides, and the claims that God has on us and all of creation. This recognition serves as a basis for making requests of God. We call on God to remain present with us and to offer us aid, strength, guidance, hope, and other provisions. But as we make requests of God in prayer, recall God's promise to abide with us, and become more cognizant of God's gracious hand in our lives, we live with deeper appreciation. Orienting us toward God and the things of God, prayer heartens us to be thankful as it keeps us aware of what God's grace truly means for our lives. Our gratitude, in turn, helps us live in ways more pleasing to God, more centered in God's purposes, and more generous toward others.

Think of it this way. A grateful heart helps keep one's eyes on God and the things of God. In recalling the psalmist's declaration, Calvin says that "they whose eyes God has opened surely learn it by heart, that in his light they may see light (Ps. 36:9)."[3] Prayer draws our attention to God's "light" certainly so that we may "see" it, but especially so that we may live as those illumined by it and grateful for it.

Benefit—Solidarity with God and Others

Prayer also has a unifying effect. Intimacy and unity go hand in hand. Prayer unites us with God, other individuals, and larger communities. Prayer joins us with God in that through it we approach God, cling to God, petition God for what we need, await God's provision, and orient ourselves toward God's purposes. Helping us relate to God in these ways, prayer also puts us in solidarity with God. Through prayer we collaborate (literally, we colabor) with God to achieve God's purposes. As Barth suggests, "It is prayer that puts us in rapport with God and permits us to collaborate with him. God wishes us to live with him, and we on our side reply, 'Yes, Father, I wish to live with thee.' And then he says, 'Pray, call me; I am listening to you. I shall live and reign with you.'"[4] Collaboration with God keeps us in solidarity with God, not only for our own sakes but also for the sake of the world.

> How very good and pleasant it is when kindred live together in unity!
>
> Psalm 133:1

Prayer also puts us in solidarity with other persons, including larger communities, as it unites us with them. I served as pastor of a congregation in metropolitan New York City on September 11, 2001, a day whose tragic events will always be remembered. My community and extended church family lost several beloved members that day, losses whose sting we still feel. However, in the aftermath of the attacks around the United States that day, I lost count of the times when I witnessed people praying—alone and with others—and feeling that somehow, in some way, these acts made a difference. I heard from people in my own congregation, but also from many people beyond it, how calling on God in prayer, in solitude and in the presence of others, led to stronger bonds, greater intimacy, deeper trust, and fewer burdens. I recall one person's saying a few weeks after this horrible event, "I never understood what a difference prayer makes before now. But somehow, it does make a difference in how you look at life, in good times and in bad ones. You don't feel so alone. You get the sense that you walk hand in hand with so many others, and that it's what we all need." Her words bear a striking similarity to ones offered by numerous others who looked at prayer differently from the way they had before.

This person was pointing to one of the foremost benefits of prayer. Whether we pray with other individuals, with the larger church, or by ourselves in solitude, we experience a unique connection with God and other human beings. The unity that we experience with other people happens by virtue of shared faith in Christ. Shared faith has roots in the bonds of baptism and takes shape throughout life as a result of entrusting our lives to God and of following Jesus *together* (Rom. 6:5). Following Jesus requires shared faith. Following Jesus happens—it must happen—with others, including not only those with whom we share a spiritual closeness but also those with whom we are in close physical proximity.

As Bonhoeffer reminds us, "the physical presence of other Christians is a source of incomparable joy and strength to the believer."

Dietrich Bonhoeffer, *Dietrich Bonhoeffer Works*, vol. 5, *Life Together/Prayerbook of the Bible*, ed. Geffrey B. Kelly, trans. Daniel W. Bloesch and James H. Burtness (1999; repr., Minneapolis: Fortress Press, 2005), 29.

Another point to stress here is that while shared faith involves praying for and with one another in the presence of God, which increases intimacy, shared faith and prayer also involve asking explicitly that God's will and purposes come to pass. Recalling the familiar words of the Lord's Prayer, Christians must join with one another in praying to God, "Thy kingdom come, thy will be done, on earth as it is in heaven." This primary focus on God, within the bounds of the common life of faith, sets the stage for our then turning attention to prayers of petition—to asking God to provide for ourselves and for others. Praying for and with one another in a central act of shared faith has marked a common life for Christians since the church's beginning.[5] In fact, no faith practice has a more prominent place in common Christian life. Jesus' earliest followers recognized what the ancient Israelites before them and Jesus himself had known, namely, that one cannot live in deep relationship to God or others without a disciplined life of prayer. Hence the apostle Paul urged those who followed Jesus to "pray without ceasing" (1 Thess. 5:17).

Solidarity with God that places us in solidarity with others has additional positive effects on the life of faith—additional benefits. This solidarity serves as a basis for hospitality toward members of the faith community but also toward those beyond it. Following the events of September 11, one noticed a marked improvement in people's collective patience, warmth, and generosity, and in their overall dispositions toward one another. This improvement was true in the congregation I served on Long Island but also in the larger community. Although not typically thought of as an overly warm, hospitable, or patient place, even the city of New York projected a different tone of life. I believe that large groups of people praying with and for one another,

and for the world, played a significant role in this change.
In my own congregation, I noticed parishioners developing
greater awareness and interest in the well-being not only of
themselves and their fellow church members—though this
was certainly evident—but of larger segments of the human
community and the world at large. As one person remarked
in a board meeting, "Widespread suffering, especially when
it hits so close to home, opens your eyes to things you don't
usually notice or think that much about. It has a way of
making you feel like we're all much more alike than we are
different." This remark takes on added meaning as we recall
that perhaps the most widely known Scripture verse, John
3:16, declares that "God so loved the world." This means
that God loves everyone, all of creation, and therefore that
those who live in solidarity with God must extend hospitality on God's behalf. The church must never look only at
itself; it must also look out to a world in need. Colaboring
with God requires this.

At the same time, we must not forget that prayer fosters a kind of hospitality, generosity, and interest that issue
in mutual concern, care, and nurture *within* the community
of faith. Promoting hospitality among its members, prayer
helps us attend to one another's needs, share life's burdens,
and also celebrate life's joys. To put it another way, prayer
fosters mutual dependence among those who pray
together. Prayer does this because it draws our gaze not
only toward God but also toward one another. In drawing
us to both, prayer keeps before us God's unwavering concern for all people. A prayerful approach to life also keeps
us aware of the gospel imperative that we love one another
as Christ has loved us.[6] As the author of 1 John puts it, "If
we love one another, God lives in us, and his love is per-

fected in us" (1 John 4:12). Love for God and love for our neighbor remain inseparable. Through this love we discover and rediscover not only our need for God but also our fundamental need for others and their need for us.

This mutual dependence, in turn, fosters a related benefit of prayer, namely, appropriate humility. It does so by guarding against tendencies to "go it alone" in life or to believe that we singularly sustain ourselves. Robert Schuller, a well-known preacher and advocate of "possibility thinking" and its close cousin, a "gospel of prosperity," wrote a book that endorses living with the following life maxim: "If it's going to be, it's up to me."[7] He touts self-reliance and self-sufficiency as central virtues for the Christian life. Although he recognizes that we also can and must rely on God and others, his primary focus remains personal responsibility and action—what we can do for ourselves in order to "do what we want" and "achieve anything."[8] I find that a significant number of people that I speak with about prayer hold a somewhat similar view.

Praying for and with one another, in shared solidarity with God, encourages living with a different life maxim, namely, "If it's going to be, it's up to God, me, and those who help to support and sustain me in the shared life of faith." This approach doesn't make for as catchy a book title, but I believe that it reflects more accurately how God calls those who follow Jesus to live. Luke describes how Jesus' earliest followers shared their lives with one another when he says, "All who believed were together and had all things in common" (Acts 2:44). Moreover, the Bible repeatedly urges mutual dependence and reliance. These qualities reveal themselves when we share our joys as well as our burdens; when we form and maintain relationships that buoy us during times of struggle and despair; when we create bonds of friendship, brotherhood, and sisterhood; and when we deepen our ties to the community of faith.[9] I cannot overemphasize the importance of viewing faith in terms of life together in community, especially when so much of what is said, written, and practiced in the Christian life issues from an attitude of "If it's going to be, then it's up to me." Prayer helps to form and sustain community by keeping a shared focus on the gifts of solidarity with God and others—in and through Jesus Christ—and on the God-given responsibility and joy that comes with it.

> Christianity means community through Jesus Christ and in Jesus Christ.
>
> Bonhoeffer, *Dietrich Bonhoeffer Works*, 31.

Benefit—Faithfulness to Jesus' Example

The Bible describes Jesus as the one in whom "all the fullness of God was pleased to dwell" (Col. 1:19). At the core of a faithful Christian life lies the goal of looking at this Jesus and seeking to be like him—the one in whom we glimpse God. Our own lives reflect this "fullness of God" as we seek to act, love, and hope as Jesus did. The Christian life, therefore, has everything to do with following Jesus' example. Throughout the Gospels, which bear witness to Jesus' life, we observe him saying to those who will listen, "Follow me!"[10] In this invitation, we find the most basic requirement for a faithful life—following Jesus.

> Jesus said, "If you know me, you will know my Father also. From now on you do know him and have seen him."
>
> John 14:6–7

Note further that Jesus calls people to follow him in every facet of life, including joy and celebration, suffering and regret; in love for God, but also in love for others and for oneself; in generosity, personal sacrifice, solidarity with God, and steadfast devotion to God's will, purposes, and vision for the world. Calling people to himself, Jesus points out that the essence of the faithful life is knowing Jesus. We need look no further than to Jesus and his life in order to see how God calls us to live. At the same time, Jesus has confidence that his call to follow will be heeded: "'My sheep hear my voice. I know them, and they follow me'" (John 10:27). In the New Testament and in the present age, we witness people responding faithfully to Jesus' invitation. At our best, we respond faithfully as well.

Despite its unfortunate commercialization in recent years, the question "What would Jesus do?" remains at the heart of the Christian life. We cannot ask ourselves a more pertinent question than this one as we seek intimacy and solidarity with God, and as we strive to live faithfully as followers of Jesus. But we also must ask these related questions: How would Jesus love? Whom would Jesus love and associate with? How would Jesus treat other people, including those with undesirable qualities? What would Jesus value? What kind of forgiveness and forbearance would Jesus practice? What would Jesus give up for the sake of another in need? How would Jesus live in a world of limited resources and practice good stewardship of the earth? How would Jesus respond to injustice, violence, and neglect, both when these take place between or among individuals and when they occur on a more systemic or structural level? Recalling the well-known title of a book by the medieval monk Thomas à Kempis, these questions and others like them suggest that along with following Jesus, the Christian life requires no less than "the imitation of Christ."[11] As we have noted, Luther took this idea a step further, suggesting that following Christ requires that we become a "little Christ" for others. Perhaps we best approach the Christian life in terms of seeking to become what Luther suggests.

So how might we do this? One way is through living a more prayerful life. Actually, we find no better way of heeding the call to follow and imitate Christ—of keeping in mind the types of questions that point us toward Jesus and hold up his example—than through the regular practice of prayer. And how specifically does prayer help? Prayer aids us in these matters because it keeps us mindful of the *decision* we have made to follow Jesus.

What will I say when Jesus invites *me* to follow him?

To follow anyone or anything involves a decision. Assuming that we have freedom in the matter, we must elect to follow or not. The choice is ours. Following Jesus is no exception. Having heard his call to follow him, we must choose whether and how we will respond. Will we follow, or not? If we follow, what will this involve? Furthermore, what might keep us from following, whether immediately or down the road? Facing these questions, we are no different from Peter, Levi, the rich young ruler, and all the others that Jesus invited to follow him. He called out to them saying, "Follow me," and they were left to answer.

Prayer offers help for following and imitating Jesus in that it keeps us mindful of our own answer to Jesus' call. Specifically, in prayer we set aside whatever distracts attention to Jesus' invitation—and to Jesus' example—while also daring to ask ourselves honestly whether we, in our own lives, give evidence of following him. Do we look to Jesus first when seeking to live the faithful life? Or do we look elsewhere? To what extent does our choice to follow Jesus affect what we prize, the goals that we set and work to achieve, the decisions that we make, the degree to which we love, or how we interact with others, whether friend or foe? In a nutshell, how does our commitment to God made apparent in following Jesus Christ serve as the basis for all of life? These kinds of questions, which we may pay close attention to in prayer, remind us not only of Jesus' gracious invitation to follow him but also of the decision we have made to do so *and* what this decision involves, presently and throughout the rest of our lives.

I should state explicitly here what has been implicitly noted thus far, namely, that following Jesus requires *obedience*. As Bonhoeffer points out, when it comes to following Jesus, our only choices are obedience or disobedience. Therefore, faith (or belief) in Christ and obedience to Christ remain inseparable.[12] We cannot have one without the other. Furthermore, we demonstrate obedience as much by what we do, how we live, how we treat others, and what we set our hopes on as by what we believe, confess, or proclaim with words. Many people think that they must first believe rightly (orthodoxy) before they can live rightly (orthopraxis). Some traditions even use the term "believer" to denote the core identity of the one who follows Jesus. But if we're not careful, this approach can mistakenly separate what must stay joined together, namely, what we believe and how we act. In fact, Bonhoeffer goes as far as to say that, although discipleship consists of an unwavering commitment to Christ tied to what we believe about him, answering Jesus' call to follow involves deeds more than words and action over mere thought, admiration, or even confession of faith.[13] Such a perspective grows out of the biblical wisdom that "faith without works is ... dead" (Jas. 2:26) and that Jesus' followers must "be doers of the word" (Jas. 1:22).

> We actually have to *learn* to believe in God; it doesn't just happen on its own.

Moreover, Bonhoeffer links belief in God to following Jesus for another reason. For Bonhoeffer, a first step in following Jesus involves putting ourselves in a situation where we can believe and where faith can begin, and this new situation differs from our previous one, before we believed. Citing the examples of Levi and Peter, Bonhoeffer writes,

> The first step puts the follower into the situation of being able to believe. If people do not follow, they remain behind, then they do not learn to believe. ... As long as Levi sits in the tax collector's booth and

Peter at his nets, they would do their work honestly and loyally, they would have old or new knowledge of God. But if they want to learn to believe in God, they have to follow the Son of God incarnate and walk with him.[14]

In other words, we learn to believe by making a *commitment* to learning. We make this commitment by entrusting our very lives—all that we have and are—to the One we have recognized as Lord and decided to follow. The object of our commitment is Jesus. We learn to believe, and we believe more strongly, by living in obedience to him.

The concept of obedience may conjure up negative thoughts and feelings in you. Most of us live amid cultures where obedience garners suspicion. For example, you may associate obedience with immaturity and a lack of self-empowerment and self-dignity. Moreover, due to a history of abuses that followed from people remaining obedient to those who misused power and breached trust, hearing that obedience stands front and center in the Christian life may prove challenging if not a bit disheartening. I have indeed spoken with many people who live encumbered and distressed lives that are tied in some way to having been "obedient" to misguided, even abusive, persons, institutions, or ideals—people who have conformed their own lives accordingly. But obedience and conformity to Christ involves freedom, not confinement; unbounded love, not abuse. Says Jesus,

"The Spirit of the Lord is upon me,
  because he has anointed me to bring good news to the
  poor.

He has sent me to proclaim release to the captives
   and recovery of sight to the blind, to let the oppressed
      go free."

                                    Luke 4:18

Living obediently to Jesus, his example, and his charge to those who follow involves something altogether different from misplaced obedience to those who abuse, neglect, or injure. In obedience to Christ we experience God's most profound love and concern. As a result, we find the freedom truly to live.

> For freedom Christ has set us free. Stand firm, therefore, and do not submit again to a yoke of slavery.
>
>   Galatians 5:1

Prayer helps us recall this freedom, for in prayer we remember that we have signed on to follow Jesus. We also take notice that this decision requires living in obedience to him and allowing our lives to be patterned accordingly. Prayer thus invites us in our distracted lives to pay closer attention to what God has offered in Christ. Says Calvin, "So true it is that we dig up by prayer the treasures that were pointed out by the Lord's gospel, and which our faith has gazed upon."[15] Prayer draws our attention to these treasures that we experience most profoundly in the life that imitates Jesus. Perhaps the author of 1 Peter best sums up the goal of deciding to follow Jesus and seeking to remain faithful to his example: "Come to him, a living stone, though rejected by mortals yet chosen and precious in God's sight, and like living stones, let yourselves be built into a spiritual house, to be a holy priesthood, to offer spiritual sacrifices acceptable to God through Jesus Christ" (1 Pet. 2:4–5).

A PRAYER FOR YOU TO PRAY

(Prepare yourself to pray by getting yourself still, taking a few breaths, and opening yourself up to God.)

> Bless the LORD, O my soul,
>   and all that is within me,
>   bless [God's] holy name.
> Bless the LORD, O my soul,
>   and do not forget all [God's] benefits.
>   Psalm 103:1–2

These words from Scripture remind us, O God, that you offer benefits to those who love you. You invite us through prayer into a close and intimate relationship with you. In prayer, you stand with us throughout life, such that we are never alone. You also help us, as we pray, to be more like Jesus and to live as he did. Thank you, Lord, for these gracious gifts. Help me and all people to live more worthy of them. I ask this through Jesus Christ. Amen.

Chapter 4

WITH WHOM DO WE PRAY?

"For where two or three are gathered in my name, I am there among them."

Matthew 18:20

For some people, praying alone feels peaceful and helpful while praying with others feels uncomfortable and problematic. As a matter of fact, to the extent that they practice prayer, many people say that it feels sufficiently satisfying to pray on their own. Not only do they sense no need to join with others in this "chief exercise of faith," but often they find the prospects of interpersonal or group prayer unappealing if not intimidating. Furthermore, even among so-called "church people," meaning those who spend a good deal of time engaged in the life and ministry of a congregation, praying with other people outside of a worship service can seem optional and perhaps altogether unnecessary.

THE COMMON APPEAL OF "PRIVATE" FAITH

This ambivalence about praying with other people often relates to the widespread assumption that the most sacred aspect of life, and especially religious life, is *privacy*.[1] As one of the most "personal" facets of our way of life, the thinking goes, a person's faith is best kept private—meaning, in this case, between oneself and God. Accordingly, when opportunities arise to talk about faith (e.g., through testimony) or to practice one's faith more publicly (e.g., through acts of interpersonal prayer), many people hesitate to use these opportunities. These practices seem awkward and, for some people, even impolite. Faith, they say, is better kept undisclosed.

I'm reminded here of one person's remark several years ago, when I served as a pastor. She had obvious personal gifts for ministry, and she maintained a high degree of involvement in congregational life. Bright, interesting, and open-minded, she presented as among the more outgoing and approachable members, seeming to draw others to herself with relative ease. I would call her a natural leader with an infectious personality. Most of her involvement in church life centered on common meals and various mission and outreach endeavors. Referring to herself as a "doer," she had planned and hosted numerous events, some of them quite complicated logistically and most of which involved very public efforts: advertising, recruiting other members to help, and even writing pieces for the church newsletter. Her facility with all of this came as no surprise to me, for she appeared to enjoy forming and building relationships and joining with others in acts of service. She carried herself as a very "public" person and seemed to thrive in group settings.

Although her contributions to the congregation's life and mission were already significant and certainly appreciated, I wanted to encourage her to make even greater use of her talents. So I inquired about her interest in leading a weekly Bible study and prayer group that was dwindling. She was just the kind of leader this group needed to reenergize them, I thought. So I asked if she would consider taking this on. Her immediate, unchecked response to my query was "Oh I could never do that. I'm really a private person . . . especially when it comes to my faith."

I had heard similar responses before—many, in fact. And although I admit to feeling somewhat disappointed to hear this from her, she simply indicated what many others would recognize in their faith communities and, perhaps, in their own lives. When it comes to prayer, a significant number of people prefer a more private and solitary approach. They view prayer almost entirely in terms of relating one-on-one to God, and they tend to think that this relationship happens best as they retreat from others and, usually, from the demands of everyday life. Even people who seem quite "public" in other expressions of their faith, such as working to head up mission projects or outreach efforts, sometimes think of acts like prayer as essentially private matters. In fact, they may even view this tack as the most "spiritual" or "devout" way, as evidenced by another person's comment to me: "What I find so helpful about prayer is that when I pray, it's just me and God." Perhaps you feel this way, too.

JESUS' ALTERNATIVE APPROACH

Let's remember that Jesus lived with a different view of the faithful life. He also modeled an alternative approach to prayer. Although his life included moments of retreat and solitude, one-on-one time with God, he gave much more time and attention to sharing his life and faith with others. Jesus never separated acts of prayer from his public ministry. He invited people to pray and taught them how (Matt. 6:5–14; 7:7–11; Luke 11:1–13). He prayed with and on behalf of others (Luke 9:28–29; Mark 14:32–33; John 17:20–23). When praying in solitude, he nevertheless remained tethered to his people as he kept God's will for himself and them in mind. Neither his praying nor his faith was kept private. In fact, these never unfolded apart from deep interpersonal and public commitments that others could witness. These included people who did not know him as well as those that he called to remain by his side, share his life, and work with him on God's behalf. We might go as far as to identify Jesus' life and faith as "devout" precisely because of their essentially interpersonal and public natures.

> Jesus did not look at prayer as something to be kept to himself.

We see from Jesus' example that faithfulness requires sharing our lives with others, especially our faith and its practices. Faithfulness involves *common* commitments to God and to God's purposes. It entails acting and praying *with* other people. It involves *mutual* goals of embodying God's love and hope and imparting these generously and widely. As Jesus pointed out, like different branches united by their dependency on the same one vine to flourish, those who follow Jesus—by virtue of their reliance on him—remain united, bound together, and necessarily engaged in *common* life. "Apart from me," he says, "you can do nothing" (John 15:5).

I interpret Jesus words as conveying something like this: "Don't live apart from me; live close to me! Live close to me by living as I did." If so, this suggests that we should not look at prayer or any other benefit of faith as something that involves merely ourselves and God. Rather, the faithful life, which we live bound to Jesus and his example, calls for holding these benefits in common and partaking of them *together*.

THE BODY AND ITS MEMBERS

Recall also these well-known words that Jesus spoke to his disciples: "'Where two or three are gathered in my name, I am there among them'" (Matt. 18:20). He made this statement when speaking of life in the *community* of faith—the church. In question was how members should relate to one another when grievances occur. What should happen after one "sins" against another, such that the fabric of the shared life becomes stressed if not torn? Jesus answers this question first by conveying his assumption that those offended will seek reconciliation, even if this requires multiple attempts. He then details how to seek this (Matt. 18:15–20).

At its heart, attempt at reconciliation, which must mark the Christian life, requires inviting the presence, witness, and support of other members. When offenses (sins) occur among those who follow him, Jesus points out that neither these transgressions nor their repair involves merely the offended and offending parties. Rather, the larger community plays a central role because it is affected. As the apostle Paul described a community that forms to follow Jesus, it makes up "one body," a living organism consisting of interconnected and interdependent parts (members) that suffer, receive honor, and rejoice with one another.[2] Whatever occurs among some members affects all the others.

Most of us, I suspect, will understand what Paul had in mind when depicting the church as one body with interconnected parts. We have witnessed in our own lives what he claimed about interdependency. As people live together, share commitments, embrace common ideals, and work alongside each other; as they struggle, disagree, and have to rely on one another—in other words, as people share their lives—their relationships become intertwined. These

involve give-and-take, a degree of reciprocity and mutuality.
Whether thinking about congregations, families of origin,
extended families, classrooms, the workplace, professional
organizations, civic clubs, or any other group, the experiences, status, and well-being of any one member or a few
usually has a noticeable effect on the others.

> For just as the body is one and has many members, and all
> the members of the body, though many, are one body, so it
> is with Christ.
>
> 1 Corinthians 12:12

Note further that the approaches Jesus and Paul
advocate mirror what Jesus indicated elsewhere concerning
his desire for interconnectedness among his followers. In
prayer to God on behalf of his disciples, he asked "that they
may all be one . . . as we are one, I in them and you in me,
that they may be completely one, so that the world may
know that you have sent me and have loved them even as
you have loved me" (John 17:20–23). Jesus recognized that
his followers live with unique and strong connections—to
him, to God, *and* to one another. As Luke understood
them, people of "the Way," as early Christians were called,
lived bound together *because* they signed on to follow
Jesus.[3] He was the basis for these relationships, and he provided the model for relating.

> The whole group of those who believed were of one heart
> and soul.
>
> Acts 4:32

In a similar vein, Paul wrote of his desire for the Christians in Colossae: "I want their hearts to be encouraged and united in love, so that they may have all the riches of assured understanding and have the knowledge of God's mystery, that is, Christ himself, in whom are hidden all the treasures of wisdom and knowledge" (Col. 2:2).[4] These and various other Scripture passages that point to the collective nature of the Christian life indicate that it cannot be a private affair. We could go as far as to say that whatever virtues the qualities of retreat and solitude have, whether for prayer or anything else, they have these virtues only because the *community* of faith holds priority status. Our place in the body of Christ allows for one-on-one time with God, and we may feel free to practice our faith accordingly. But we should never mistake this benefit for what lies at the heart of following Jesus—namely, membership in the *body*. As the apostle Paul put it, "Now you are the body of Christ, and individually members of it" (1 Cor. 12:27).

So whenever you catch yourself gravitating more toward private faith and less toward collective faith, remember that the earliest followers of Jesus recognized that he *lives* among those gathered *together* in his name and that his presence makes those who follow him *one*. Not only this, but according to Jesus, the community made one in him does no less than bear witness to God's love—love for Jesus, love for those who follow him, and love for the world (John 17:20–23).

BENEFITS OF CORPORATE PRAYER

The practice of corporate or interpersonal prayer helps diminish whatever inklings one may have toward a more privatized faith or spiritual life.[5] This type of prayer calls on us to broaden our life gaze to include others along with ourselves and to recognize that we live faithfully as Jesus' disciples to the extent that we follow his example and serve others on his behalf *together*. But what else might we say about this way of praying? I have suggested that followers of Jesus pray for three principal reasons: God has acted graciously; Jesus invited prayer; and the Holy Spirit empowers prayer. Therefore, let us keep in mind that the chief *ends* of prayer, whether practiced in solitude or community, remain these: communion with God, fidelity to Christ, and shared life in the Spirit. Nevertheless, prayer serves other invaluable objectives, which we also may think of as God's benefits that come with the life of faith (Ps. 103:2). Specifically, prayer keeps us mindful of the bond that we have with others who follow Jesus. Likewise, by virtue of this bond, which remains the basis of shared faith and life, prayer practiced in community shapes *individual* and *collective* lives in particular ways.

We may think of the bonding and shaping effects of prayer in terms of five related benefits tied to praying in community:

1. Prayer promotes capacities for intention, attention, and reflection.
2. Prayer draws us deeper into the Christian story.
3. Prayer reminds us of who we are as followers of Jesus—of our shared identity in Christ.
4. In prayer we recall how God in Christ calls us to live, paying particular attention to cultivating "spiritual fruit" and seeking to exemplify these in our lives.
5. Prayer encourages us to share and bear one another's burdens.

Let us consider each of these benefits of praying in community.

Benefit—Prayer Promotes Intention, Attention, and Reflection

Prayer fosters three capacities among both individuals and communities: *intention, attention,* and *reflection.*[6] These capacities contribute to greater awareness and understanding of God and of one another, to greater self-awareness and self-understanding, *and* to living more strongly tied to each of these.

Intention relates to interest, motivation, and purpose. To act with intention toward anyone or anything involves proceeding with resolve. This stems from a degree of desire and typically relates to some end goal. For example, if I act intentionally to read the Bible every day, we can assume that I have interest and motivation to read it, and that I'm purposeful in this regard. In other words, I have made a conscious effort toward reading the Bible every day.

Attention essentially follows from intention, such that we focus more keenly on the object of our interest, motivation, or purpose. At the same time, we make an effort to limit whatever would distract us from this focus. If I give my attention to reading the Bible, I concentrate on it, and I attempt to keep other matters out of mind. The Scriptures receive my fullest possible consideration.

Reflection follows from intention and attention. To reflect involves reconsidering the object of intention and attention. Moreover, reflection entails thinking in a deliberate and deep manner about this object. When people reflect on something, they usually ponder it with some degree of scrutiny. For example, reflection on my practice of reading the Bible every day could consist of recalling what I have read (and also my practice of reading), thinking about its meaning, and perhaps considering ways that it challenges me with regard to several matters. These could include my views about God, Jesus, and the Spirit; my interests, values, and goals; the way that I conduct myself; or my approach to the meaning of life, the nature of forgiveness, or my relationships. In other words, the richest and most beneficial daily practice of reading the Bible requires my intention, attention, and reflection.

The same holds true for prayer. The richest experiences of praying and the most meaningful prayer life will involve consistent and concentrated intention, attention, and reflection on our parts. In turn, these will foster the greatest benefits that follow from prayer. But note too that prayer actually serves to deepen the very capacities needed to experience it to the fullest. As we pray, we cultivate the intention, attention, and reflection that we most want and need in order to enjoy the benefits of the prayerful life. How does prayer help in this way? Metaphorically speaking, it serves as a "container" of sorts for collecting and holding our intention, attention, and reflection, especially as these relate explicitly to our faith. Or think of it this way. Prayer draws us to a "place"—one with spiritual, emotional, relational, and even physical qualities—that differs in degree, and sometimes in kind, from the other "places" we live.

When we pray, we enter a separated place—a container or holding environment, if you will—where we have a unique opportunity (freedom) to be intentional, attentive, and reflective in the presence of God. Bracketing the demands, expectations, and sometimes questionable values and goals that vie for our attention if not our devotion in other places, prayer frees us to devote ourselves to God,

Jesus, and the Spirit, and to live as Jesus' followers. In a sense, praying takes us to a place that makes the Christian faith an unmatched (and less impeded) focus and object of interest. When we pray, we may let go of whatever blurs our focus on God's leading. For as the writer of the Letter to the Colossians points out, prayer keeps one "alert" to God and the things of God (Col. 4:2).

Benefit—Prayer Draws Us Deeper into the Christian Story

Helping us live more alert to God, frequent and consistent prayer also draws us deeper and deeper into the Christian story, so that it becomes the principal story by which we live. What does this mean? The Christian faith can be thought of in terms of a story.[7] For those who follow Jesus, it's a *true* story, but a story nonetheless. Specifically, it's the story of God's creative, transformative, and redemptive acts throughout history, which Christians have most frequently recognized in the history of Israel; the life, death, and resurrection of Jesus; and the ongoing work of the Holy Spirit. Seeking to follow Jesus and live the Christian life requires orientation to this story, which we encounter in the Bible and the historic practices of the church. As we accept God's invitation into the Christian story—as we sign on to follow Jesus—we become increasingly shaped, guided, and motivated by it. Its norms, values, challenges, and promises become more and more our own. This story tells of God's nature and character. It conveys what God has done for us and for the world in Christ. It tells about how the Holy Spirit keeps us in relationship to God and one another through Christ. This story also suggests how we might respond to God's gracious initiative and gifts by living in particular ways, the ways that Jesus himself lived. We discover all that this story means and what it can mean *for us and others* precisely because we have become part of it.

I stress that we *first* become part of the Christian story, and *only then* does it touch our personal stories. The Christian story takes us into itself by the power of the Spirit before we can ever take it into ourselves—that is, into our personal stories. In other words, personal stories get drawn into its larger, farther-reaching, and encompassing story. It's not the case that we invite the Christian story into our lives in order to map it onto the stories already valued and operative there (e.g., our personal stories of family, career, successes, failures, values, or goals) . Rather, our stories map onto its story. Our lives take shape by virtue of one principal life, namely, that of Jesus. *He* is the story. Therefore, his story serves as the basis for our own.

> We are different because Christ lives in us (see Gal. 2:20).

As we seek to live more explicitly from the Christian story, it increasingly encompasses our own personal stories. It "molds, guides, and sets boundaries" for our personal stories, and thus for how we live with others and engage the world on God's behalf.[8] The Christian story also alters at least some aspects of what once marked our personal stories before we signed on to follow Jesus. Why? In Paul's terms, the Christian story "transforms" us.[9] We might then think of following Jesus as essentially being taken in by the Christian story to be transformed. Personally and collectively, we want this story to encompass us and shape us, to make us different from before. We want to say, with Paul, "It is no longer I who live, but it is Christ who lives in me." (Gal. 2:20), and we allow for this to happen. In turn, our lives reflect more and more the qualities that Jesus modeled and asked his followers to embrace, whether in relationship to God or to other persons. So we never take our eyes off of Jesus' story when thinking about, living, or crafting our personal stories. We have no personal story independent from Jesus' own. As suggested in the line of a well-known hymn, to follow Jesus means that we look at his life and confess, "*This* is my story," too.[10]

Let me also stress these two related points. First, the deeper we are drawn into the Christian story, the more our lives become focused on responding to God's initiative to be God for us in Christ Jesus. Why? Because we live from the Christian story with greater intention, attention, and reflection. Furthermore, the deeper we get into the Christian story, the closer we live to Christ and the more his life and faith serve as examples for our own. Second, because prayer draws us ever deeper into the Christian story, thereby bringing us closer to Christ, prayer both encourages this response to God's initiative and serves as an agent for responding.

Benefit—Prayer Reminds Us of Our Shared Identity in Christ

"Never forget who you are," my parents would say when I was growing up. Sometimes they also said, "Never forget where you come from." With maturity came a better sense of what was behind these urgings and a better understanding of what they meant. But even as a child, I think that I got the gist of it. Who we are and where we come from remain inseparably linked, and both matter a great deal.

Our roots, history, families, relationships, experiences, beliefs, and values lie at the core of our uniqueness as people. Whether taken independently or together, these mainstay features of life inform who we are—our personal stories—and they matter so much that we should live with keen awareness of them and understand how they continue to influence us.

Although these features will change to some degree throughout life, in that personal stories continue to be crafted and recrafted by virtue of our experiences and encounters with others' personal stories, these features nevertheless remain at the core of identity. In other words, these features always shape who we *are* and *will become*. Therefore, we should recognize them and pay attention to how they figure into who we (and others) understand ourselves to be. In fact, remembering our identity (who we are) and what informs it (where we come from) remains essential throughout life. When we cease to remember these things and to pay attention to them, we lose something central and necessary to our humanity.

By drawing us deeper into the Christian story and bringing us closer to Jesus, *the* story, prayer helps us to remember who we are and from where we come. In prayer we deliberately recall Jesus and his story. We also pay closer attention to our personal stories and, most important, how these came to be by virtue of their relationship to Jesus' story. In Paul's terms, prayer keeps our focus on how the Christian story *transforms* our own stories (Phil. 3:21). But prayer helps in other ways, too. It helps us stay attuned to this transformed identity and helps keep it the basis for how we strive to live. Therefore, prayer helps us not only to recognize who we are, where we come from, and where we hope to go, but also to live in ways that are true to this identity. To put it in a different way, prayer helps prevent us from living as someone we are not.

Benefit—Prayer Cultivates Spiritual Fruit (Which Gets Shared)

Prayer offers another related benefit. Alerting us to our place in the Christian story and to our corresponding identity in Christ, prayer helps us grow in faith, hope, and love. Paul identifies these qualities, which we may call spiritual fruit, as marks of a life in Christ.[11] Those who follow Jesus live with faith, hope, and love. Each gets nurtured in prayer. These spiritual fruits also become apparent in how Jesus' followers conduct themselves. When we face hardships in life, we can appeal to the assurances of faith (Heb. 11:1). When our situation seems hopeless, we can recall that our struggles will not have the final say because of what God has promised in Christ (Rom. 5:5; 2 Cor. 1:10; 1 Tim. 4:10). When confronted with the evils that destroy life and spread violence and hatred, those who follow Jesus can seek to live in love (Rom. 5:5; 8:31–35). For as Paul assures us, "Faith, hope, and love abide" (1 Cor. 13:13).

Note further that Paul typically made reference to these three qualities together. When he spoke of one of them, he usually mentioned the others; and here again he had in mind the *collective* faith, hope, and love of the *community* that follows Jesus. For example, he wrote to the church of the Thessalonians, "We always give thanks to God for all of you and mention you in our prayers, constantly remembering before our God and Father your work of faith and labor of love and steadfastness of hope in our Lord Jesus Christ" (1 Thess. 1:1–3). The "you" refers not to individual Christians by themselves but rather to a group of Jesus' followers—the *church* gathered in a particular place. Paul recognized that individual disciples of Jesus are who they are and live the stories they live precisely because they share their lives with others who follow Jesus. Whether writing about spiritual fruit or other matters, Paul addressed the *body* of Christians first. Only then did he address individual members.

But Paul did identify numerous spiritual fruits as marks and goals of the Christian life. Other biblical writers did, too. These spiritual fruits include faith, hope, and love, and also others. Let us take a closer look at several of these and then consider how prayer in community helps to cultivate them. We begin by drawing from letters to the churches in Colossae and Galatia. Although we find mention of various fruits of the Christian life elsewhere, these two letters provide enough to guide us in our thinking about what these benefits of faith look like, and also how to go about nurturing them in ourselves and others.

The letter to the Colossians opens with Paul expressing gratitude to the Christians in Colossae for their demonstrations of faith, hope, and love. He writes,

> In our prayers for you we always thank God, the Father of our Lord Jesus Christ, for we have heard of your faith in Christ Jesus and of the love that you have for all the saints, because of the hope laid up for you in heaven. You have heard of this hope before in the word of truth, the gospel, that has come to you. Just as it is bearing fruit and growing in the whole world, so it has been bearing fruit among yourselves from the day you heard it and truly comprehended the grace of God.
>
> Colossians 1:3–6

Paul's gratitude has spawned his prayers for the community and its shared life, wherein he gives thanks for their faith, hope, and love and identifies additional spiritual fruit that he asks God to bring forth among them:

> We have not ceased praying for you and asking that you may be filled with the knowledge of God's will in all spiritual wisdom and understanding, so that you may lead lives worthy of the Lord, fully pleasing to him, as you bear fruit in every good work and as you grow in the knowledge of God. May you be made strong with all the strength that comes from his glorious power, and may you be prepared to endure everything with patience, while joyfully giving thanks to the Father, who has enabled you to share in the inheritance of the saints in the light.
>
> Colossians 1:9–12

These passages signal a relationship between gratitude, prayer, and particular qualities joined to a faithful life. In giving thanks to God, one may pray for growth in matters like faith, love, and hope; in knowledge of God's will; in spiritual wisdom and understanding; and for living as those who please God. One may also pray for strength, endurance, patience, and joy as one follows Jesus. Paul prays for these things. He asks these things of God on others' behalf. He asks, too, that others would pray for him (Col. 4:3).[12] Presumably, one may pray for *any* spiritual fruit cited in Scripture, which includes these additional ones that Paul cites in a well-known list taken from his letter to the Galatians: joy, peace, kindness, generosity, gentleness, and self-control (Gal. 5:22–23). We can ask in prayer for what Paul asked, praying that God would cultivate similar spiritual fruit in others and in ourselves.

How exactly does prayer help to cultivate this spiritual fruit? It does so by fostering the same kind of intention, attention, and reflection previously mentioned. In prayer, we may make nurturing spiritual fruit, in ourselves and others, the principal object of concern. We may focus on opening up to the Spirit's working in us, allowing for spiritual fruit to find deeper roots and come forth in more abundant blooms. We may also pay closer attention in prayer to what we ourselves may do to promote a greater yield of this fruit in our lives. In other words, we may consider more closely how to think, feel, relate, act, and dream in ways conducive to nurturing and sustaining more faith, hope, and love, in us and in others with whom we live. Ideally, we learn to focus on these benefits beyond the context of prayer as well; and a consistent practice of praying lends itself to this learning. Moreover, spiritual fruit gets cultivated in ways other than prayer, such as through the practices of worship, membership in a faith community, reading Scripture, serving others, and confession.[13] Nevertheless, as the "chief exercise of faith," we must recognize prayer as an indispensable way to remember God's benefits (Ps. 103:2) found in spiritual fruit *and* to seek after these, particularly those that come with following Jesus in community.

Benefit—Sharing and Bearing One Another's Burdens

I want to make mention of one more benefit of praying in community, that of encouragement to share and bear one another's burdens. Of course, prayer encourages the sharing of joys and celebrations, too. In fact, a life of prayer in community fosters sharing the whole range of life experiences. But the Scriptures indicate the particular importance of sharing one another's difficulties and relying on one another for support (Rom. 15:1–7; Gal. 6:2). We give this mutual support through prayer. As we pray, we may look to others, and they may look to us, for help with cultivating spiritual fruit, and especially for living with a degree of faith, hope, and love that we could not muster without one another. Prayer in community fosters reliance on one another in a manner and to a degree that provide what mere self-reliance cannot offer. Through "bearing one another's burdens" (Gal. 6:2), we gain a different perspective on what we face in life and more resolve to face it. At the center of this perspective lie the faith, hope, and love that we enjoy through the bonds of the Christian story.

I was reminded of this benefit of prayer by a former student, Pamela, as I wrote this very chapter. Telling me about her recent cancer diagnosis, surgery, and ongoing treatment, she said,

> It has been a good lesson . . . that there really aren't seasons of all bad or all good things, but the good and the bad travel on parallel tracks. I decided at the beginning of my illness that I wouldn't burden myself with the need to rely on *my* faith—it's kind of hard to muster in the midst of illness anyway, and I didn't want to "talk myself into" being some kind of victim of not having "enough" faith if I didn't get better. Instead, I asked my friends to allow me to rely on *their* faith to "lower me through the roof to Jesus" [Mark 2:4; Luke 5:18–19]. It turned out to be a really helpful way for me—and my friends—to think about prayer during this time.

As she shared her experience with me, I sensed that something remarkable had happened, not only in her life but in her friends' lives, too. Like the paralytic who leaned on others and their faith for help when getting to Jesus, Pamela leaned on her friends. She allowed them to share her burdens. Moreover, just as those near the paralytic went to great ends to support him, even cutting a hole in the roof and lowering him to Jesus, Pamela's friends had, through their prayers, done the same for her. They willingly, and from what I gather, gladly, shared her burdens. Their faith allowed her not to have to rely on her faith alone. Pamela had faith, too. I'm sure of it. And we should not discount its importance. But her great wisdom showed itself in her recognition that it's not simply one's own faith that sustains. It's not merely our own, singular, private faith that puts us with Jesus but instead the collective faith that we share with others. Praying from this kind of faith, moreover, carries us when we cannot carry ourselves. Pamela understood this well, and in leaning on her friends and their faith and prayers, she has something to teach us all.

Through joining together in prayer for healing and peace, Pamela and her friends helped cultivate for each other faith, hope, and love—spiritual fruit tied to the faith that they share and live together. I sensed, too, that this faith, hope, and love spawned other fruit: more patience for living with uncertainty; greater joy over not having to encounter illness alone or watch a friend encounter it alone; increased offers of kindness and generosity, which illness can bring about because it reminds us of the fragility of life and of what matters most; and perhaps a "gentleness" toward oneself, others, and life itself, a gentleness whose value we often recognize most clearly as we come face-to-face with the harshness of disease. Pamela's experience shows us what can and does happen as we pray with and for others who share the desire to follow Jesus: We are "built up" in our faith (Jude 1:20).

WHAT ABOUT PRAYING BY YOURSELF?

Of course, a focus on praying with others does not mean that praying by yourself, in solitude, has little value. It has great value. We need look no further than to Jesus to have this confirmed. As noted previously, Jesus prayed with others *and* by himself. At times he even separated himself from others to spend time alone in prayer, and sometimes for long stretches.[14] He also noted how praying by yourself can help keep your full attention on God. So do what Jesus did. Pray by yourself, and make it a regular part of your prayer life. In doing so you follow one of Jesus' examples. But remember his examples of praying with others, too, such that praying in community becomes normative and even the basis for your solitary time with God in prayer. To say it differently, think about how learning to pray with others and doing so on a regular basis can lead to the rich and meaningful practice of solitary prayer, rather than the other way around.

A PRAYER FOR YOU TO PRAY

(Prepare yourself to pray by getting yourself still, taking a few breaths, and opening yourself up to God.)

> Eternal God, you are the one in whom we live and move and have our being. Although we often live

isolated lives, thinking and operating as if following Jesus is largely an individual or private affair, his own life provides a different example. In him you have called us to live as members of one body—the body of Christ—and to grow in personal faith as we grow in shared faith with others who seek to follow Jesus. Enable me and my siblings in faith to live and serve you faithfully. This I ask in Jesus' name. Amen.

Chapter 5
HOW DO WE PRAY?

We must learn to pray.
Dietrich Bonhoeffer, *Prayerbook of the Bible*

This chapter will teach you four different ways to pray. They include praying the Lord's Prayer, praying Scripture, engaging in contemplative prayer, and participating in liturgical (or worshipful) prayer. Each approach has a long-standing place in Christian faith, and each can enrich your own prayer life and foster the benefits discussed in chapter 3. Although you will likely find some of these approaches to be a better "fit" for you than others, I urge you to give them all a try and, eventually, to consider practicing them together in your prayer regimen. You may be surprised at how praying with different approaches can help you grow in your faith.

PRAYING THE LORD'S PRAYER

Perhaps the most familiar of all Christian prayers is what we call "The Lord's Prayer."[1] A common version goes like this:

> Our Father in heaven,
>   hallowed be your name,
>   your kingdom come,
>   your will be done,
>   on earth as in heaven.

> Give us today our daily bread.
> Forgive us our sins
>   as we forgive those who sin against us.
> Save us from the time of trial
>   and deliver us from evil.
>
> For the kingdom, the power, and the glory are yours
>   now and forever. Amen.

Probably no single prayer has been uttered by Christians more than the Lord's Prayer, and for good reason. Jesus used these words when teaching his disciples about prayer: "When you pray, pray in this way" (Luke 11:2–4; Matt. 6:9–13). Calvin saw Jesus' words as providing his disciples with the right "pattern" or "form" for prayer, with a way of praying that correctly begins with attention to and praise of God and then moves to a focus on us and our needs. Says Calvin, this approach provides true freedom in prayer, for we do not have to wonder how to pray or whether we do so faithfully. Why? Because Jesus "supplies words to our lips that free our minds from all wavering," and he "prescribed a form for us in which he set forth as in a table all that he allows us to seek of him, all that is of benefit to us, all that we need ask."[2] Moreover, as Bonhoeffer said of the Lord's Prayer, "In it, every prayer is contained. Whatever enters into the petitions of the Lord's Prayer is prayed aright; whatever has no place in it, is not prayer at all. All the prayers of the Holy Scriptures are summed up in the Lord's Prayer and all are taken up into its immeasurable breadth."[3] So we can feel confident that what we pray when using the words of the Lord's Prayer takes in other words or prayers that we would offer to God.

Praying the Lord's Prayer provides additional benefits in that it reminds us of two key matters. First, all prayer should begin with recognizing the primary reason that we pray—namely, that God acts graciously toward us and that God remains the one "in whom we live, move, and have our being" (Acts 17:28). To begin to pray by uttering the words "Our Father in heaven" recognizes that God holds supreme status and power while also calling attention to the fact that God simultaneously relates to us intimately, faithfully, and with extraordinary love. When we recognize that God lives and reigns "in heaven," we attest to God's maintaining authority over all things, including our own lives. At the same time, however, in referring to God as "*Our* Father," we recognize that God is not only God for ourselves but also for others and indeed for all people. "Our" denotes a common humanity that lives under the grace of God and stands in need of God's care and provision.

Referring to God as "Father" also affirms that God stands before us (individually and collectively) as a heavenly parent, one who, like kind and nurturing "earthly" parents, provides guidance, support, aid, and unfailing love but who offers these and myriad other provisions in ways and degrees that surpass what any human parent may offer. Jesus tells a parable most often referred to as the parable of the Prodigal Son (Luke 15:11–32) to point to God's parental qualities. We affirm these qualities in our prayers when we say, "Our Father in heaven." Moreover, addressing God as "Our Father" places us in the company of Jesus, who himself spoke to God as "Father" and used the even more familiar term "Abba" ("Papa"), and who related to God in supremely intimate ways (Mark 14:36; John 10:30). Of course, in calling God "Father" we do not mean that God is human or male. Nor do we mean that God possesses only "fatherly" qualities, whatever we might say about those. We do mean, however, that God possesses qualities that issue in care, concern, nurture, provision, and love that parents (including both mothers and fathers) may offer their children, and that God offers these unceasingly. This seems to be what Jesus had in mind, too.

Approaching God in prayer as Jesus recommends, which involves seeking to relate to God as Jesus himself did, reminds us of who God is but also of who we are. As Calvin noted, we are those who live as children of God (1 John 3:1), always reliant on "the Father of mercies and God of all comfort" (2 Cor. 1:3) to provide what we cannot.[4] To put it a bit more pointedly, to pray the Lord's Prayer reminds us that God is God and that we are not!

The second key matter that we recall when praying the Lord's Prayer is this: Because God acts graciously toward us, we may ask (petition) God for certain things and expect that God will respond. Jesus urges us to live with just this kind of expectancy. Not only did he tell his disciples to make petitions to God in prayer; he also told them to pray persistently. God will answer our prayers and provide for our needs, Jesus assures.

"Ask, and it will be given you; search, and you will find; knock, and the door will be opened for you. For everyone who asks receives, and everyone who searches finds, and for everyone who knocks, the door will be opened."
                                    Matthew 7:7–8; Luke 11:9–10

So in praying the Lord's Prayer, we not only recognize God's graciousness; we also call out to God to invoke God's presence in our lives. This sets the stage for the sharing of our lives with God, whether this sharing involves joys and celebrations or making requests of God to provide for our needs, to meet our desires, to alleviate our fears, or to answer our questions. Calling out to God with the assurances of the Lord's Prayer also sets the stage for us to await God's response with confidence. As we have already noted, Jesus' confidence in God's inexorable presence and provision ("Ask, and it will be given to you") reaffirmed what the ancient prophets and other witnesses believed about God: "When you call upon me and come and pray to me, I will hear you. When you search for me, you will find me; if you seek me with all your heart, I will let you find me, says the LORD" (Jer. 29:13–14).[5] Just as his ancestors had, Jesus urged his followers to pray, to do so persistently, to have confidence that God answers, and to live accordingly.

Here are some ways to incorporate the Lord's Prayer into your prayer life.

Method 1. Simply pray the prayer slowly but deliberately all the way through several times. Think about the words you speak and what they mean, but don't belabor any of them. Just pray in a way that feels natural and seems right to you in expectation that the Spirit will be a part of your prayer.

Method 2. Follow the same approach, but pause for a few moments between each recitation of the prayer to "listen" for what the Spirit may "say" to you.

Method 3. Break the prayer up into segments. After praying each one, pause and reflect on what you have prayed and again listen for what the Spirit might convey. For example, you might pray "Our Father in heaven" several times and then pause to think more

deeply about what you have prayed. Or you might
pray this phrase only once before pausing. You could
also try it both ways. Then you could move to the
next line of the prayer (the first petition), which says
"Hallowed be your name" ("make your name holy")
and incorporate similar moments of pausing and
reflecting. Next, move on to additional petitions and
lines in the prayer, using a similar method. Also, you
should feel free, if you want, to limit your focus to just
one aspect of the prayer and simply recite the words
having to do with this focus numerous times. For
example, you might choose "Forgive us our sins, as
we forgive those who sin against us," if forgiveness is
something you particularly have on your mind or
heart. Or you might choose to focus on "Give us
today our daily bread" and consider particular needs
that you or others have and want God to address.
And note too that it's fine to substitute "us" with "I"
if this allows you to personalize the prayer in helpful
ways. Prayer can and should be quite personal. If you
do this, however, remember to incorporate the "us"
language, too, since this will remind you of the collective, communal nature of our relationship to God
that shapes our individual (personal) relationships
with God. Both types of encounters with God—both
sorts of relationships—remain indispensable for the
Christian life.

Method 4. This method is particularly appropriate for
praying with others.[6] It involves praying the Lord's
Prayer with different people praying various parts.
Let's say you pray with two other people. You could
be the one who begins the prayer, saying, "Our
Father in heaven," with another person then saying,

"Hallowed be your name," and with the remaining person saying, "Your kingdom come." Then, you'd take another turn, saying, "Your will be done," and the second person who spoke would say, "On earth as it is in heaven," and the third person would say, "Give us today our daily bread." This process would continue to the end of the prayer, and then it could begin again. Perhaps you'd want to pray five times through, or more, and then pause to listen, ponder, and reflect together. Or you could each take a turn in praying the entire prayer through, such that each person has the opportunity to listen to the others pray the whole Lord's Prayer and to join them in silent reflection as they do it.

Remember to breathe as you pray, too. Use the deliberative approach that we've already considered while you pray the Lord's Prayer. You might want to inhale as you say one part of the prayer and exhale as you say another part. For example, breathing in, you say, "Our Father," which could symbolize "taking God" into you or inviting God to dwell in you more deeply, and in turn to lead you to a more powerful sense of God's presence and care. And then, breathing out, you could say, "in heaven," which could symbolize your seeking the things of God, that is, heavenly things, as you give yourself (your breath) to them. A different set of words and meanings may resonate more with you, but you get the idea, I hope.

Try this: Choose one of the methods described and pray the Lord's Prayer.

Try each of these approaches, adapt them in ways that you find helpful and appropriate, and try other approaches, too. Don't get bogged down paying so close attention to your methods that you miss what these seek to foster, namely, faithful and meaningful prayer before God. If I may play off of the words spoken by Jesus, remember that, like the Sabbath, the Lord's Prayer was created for human beings, not human beings for the Lord's Prayer (Mark 2:27). In other words, use this gift that Jesus gave us in ways that seem faithful, nurturing, and life-giving to you, without worrying so much about strict rules or guidelines. I believe that Jesus would want this for you.

PRAYING SCRIPTURE

In a sense, when we pray the Lord's Prayer we simply pray words of Scripture, for it is from the New Testament that the words to this prayer come to us. We might also pray other Scriptures in conjunction with praying the Lord's Prayer. One approach could be to choose particular passages of the Bible (or even entire books of the Bible) and make these the focus of praying. You may opt for a single verse, or a collection or series of verses, and then essentially follow the three methods previously described for praying the Lord's Prayer.

Consider this example. One of the most meaningful passages of Scripture to me has been Colossians 1:19, which says this about Jesus: "In him all the fullness of God was pleased to dwell." Taking cues from the three methods, you might pray this passage in these ways. You could recite this verse several times, perhaps without pausing and thus simply focusing on the repetition itself, such that the verse essentially plays like a tape in your mind. Or you could say the verse once or twice, and then stop to reflect on it more deeply and ponder how it speaks to you and your situation. Alternatively, you might hone in on one particular word or a few words in the larger passage, like "In him," "all," "fullness," "God," "pleased," and "dwell." In doing so, you might reflect on what each word (or set of words) means to you or conjures up for you. Another way of putting it is that you can focus intently ("meditate") on a single word or two, or a series of words, and see where this takes you. Then perhaps you will want to return to praying the passage as a whole and ponder how you now understand it, experience it, appreciate it, or question it differently than you did before. Or maybe you don't want to ponder these matters just then but prefer simply to "sit" with it, more restfully, and leave it there. Remember that you can try deliberative breathing with this approach, too.

Feel free to be creative and try your own ideas about ways to incorporate Scripture in your prayers and play with those ways. Moreover, be sure to try the "praying Scripture" approach with whatever passages you wish. The goal is simply to engage in prayer through an encounter with the Christian story by way of the biblical witness.

Make Sure You Pray the Psalms

Whatever passages of Scripture you include, however, I strongly encourage frequent appeal to the book of Psalms. I'm not suggesting that other books of the Bible are less important, nor do I wish to discourage regular reading or study of them or appealing to them in your prayers. You will benefit from a consistent encounter with the breadth of Scripture, which tells the whole Christian story. We encounter this story, learn about it, and allow it to become our own principal life story as we engage the Bible and the traditions and practices of the church. So read and pray all of Scripture.

However, for several reasons, the Psalms might prove particularly helpful with this approach to prayer. First of all, these passages of Scripture address the gamut of life experiences: loss and despair, fear and worry, danger and disaster, hatred and vengeance, joy and celebration, consolation and hope. So when you pray using the words of a psalm, you speak words that resonate with your own life and experiences. In some ways, you gaze into a mirror that reflects

The Psalms "mirror life with all its ups and downs, its passions, and discouragement."

Dietrich Bonhoeffer, *Dietrich Bonhoeffer Works*, vol. 5, *Life Together/Prayerbook of the Bible*, ed. Geffrey B. Kelly, trans. Daniel W. Bloesch and James H. Burtness (1999; repr., Minneapolis: Fortress Press, 2005), 147.

back to you what you are thinking, feeling, and hoping for, and possibly even how you are acting.

Second, as Bonhoeffer points out, the individual psalms make up a collection of prayers—what we call the Psalter. As with any appropriate prayer, psalms address God directly and intimately. They invoke God's presence and care. They offer praise and thanksgiving to God. They also convey the deepest human feelings, questions, and longings, especially for God. Bonhoeffer goes as far as calling the collection of psalms the "prayer book of the Bible," noting that the Scriptures urge elsewhere that we give particular importance to psalms in our lives of faith: "'Speak to one another with psalms' (Eph. 5:19). 'Teach and admonish one another . . . and . . . sing psalms' (Col. 3:16). From ancient times in the church a special significance has been attached to the *praying of Psalms* together."[7]

Third, we have in the book of Psalms the very prayers that Jesus would have known and spoken. As a faithful Jew, Jesus would have been exposed to the Psalms and would have surely known many of them by heart. Indeed, as Bonhoeffer reminds us, "Jesus died on the cross with the words of the Psalms on his lips."[8] Not only this, but according to Bonhoeffer, "the Psalter is the vicarious prayer of Christ for his congregation," such that when we pray psalms today we pray *with* Jesus himself.[9]

Taking another cue from Bonhoeffer, I suggest that you give priority to praying the Psalter in its *entirety*, such that you begin with Psalm 1 and over the course of time at whatever pace seems right, you move through the entire collection. Of course, if you find a given psalm especially meaningful or feel as though praying it would prove particularly helpful, by all means go with it. You'll likely already have some favorites that you hold dear, and you'll almost certainly feel the same about additional ones as you pray the individual psalms more regularly and become more familiar with them. My caution here is simply that you make a random or picking-and-choosing approach to reading psalms secondary to reading through the book as a whole.

Try this for praying Scripture:

Psalm 23
The LORD is my shepherd, I shall not want.
    He makes me lie down in green pastures;
he leads me beside still waters;
    he restores my soul.
He leads me in right paths
For his name's sake.

Even though I walk through the darkest valley,
    I fear no evil;
for you are with me;
    your rod and your staff—
    they comfort me.
You prepare a table before me
    in the presence of my enemies;
you anoint my head with oil;
    my cup overflows.
Surely goodness and mercy shall follow me
    all the days of my life,
and I shall dwell in the house of the LORD
    my whole life long.

Make Sure You Memorize Scripture

Before moving to the next approach to prayer, I want to comment briefly on one related practice that will not only enrich your prayer life but also help you grow in your faith and your broader life of discipleship. It's the practice of *memorizing* Scripture.

Though seemingly a dying art, Christians do well to invest themselves in efforts to memorize biblical passages. We need to know what the Bible says, and really know it, so that what it reveals about God, humanity, and the rest of the created order become deeply part of who we understand ourselves to be and how we see the world and live in it. As pastoral theologian Deborah van Deusen Hunsinger notes, the practice of memorizing Scripture bears fruit for the Christian life in that it "can help one develop a higher quality of attention" to the biblical witness, a result being that eventually "one's personal history is informed by Scripture such that Scripture actually gives it its form."[10] In other words, memorizing Scripture helps us *internalize* the Christian story more deeply. As you memorize Scripture, it shapes, directs, sets parameters for, and even transforms your personal stories, in turn transforming the way you live your life in following Jesus for the sake of the world.[11] Hunsinger describes the value of memorizing Scripture in this way: "There is real power . . . [for those] . . . who have Scripture 'in their bones' (Jer. 20:9)."[12]

STRATEGIES FOR MEMORIZING

There are various ways to memorize things, of course, including passages from the Bible. Although you'll most likely figure out what ways work best for you, here are some suggestions:

Keep a list. Make a list of five passages that you find particularly meaningful. You might already have five in mind (or possibly more), and that's OK; but be open to discovering new passages as you read the Bible regularly and as you pray on a consistent basis. As you encounter passages that speak to you, jot them down on a "running list." When you have included five passages, begin another list. In time, you'll have several lists to refer to in your practices of memorization. You might want to sort the passages by books of the Bible, or maybe by "themes" or content-related concerns. Or perhaps you'll find it interesting and helpful to organize your lists by date, by genres of Scripture (e.g., Old Testament stories, Gospels, Epistles [Letters], Psalms, the Beatitudes [Matt. 5:1–12]), or in some other fashion that interests you and helps you keep with the practice of memorizing.

Keep your list accessible. Once you have made these lists, there are all sorts of ways to keep them accessible to you. You can write them on an index card that you keep in your wallet or pocketbook. I know someone who laminates such lists and keeps one or two with her at all times, rotating the lists periodically. Perhaps you'll want to type your lists into your cell phone or PDA for electronic retrieval whenever you want. Maybe you'll keep some or all of your lists inside your Bible, or near one of your places for praying. I know another person who includes a new Scripture passage in his lunch bag, such that before he eats his "daily bread," he incorporates the passage in his blessing and thanksgiving to God. You may have some other method in mind that will allow you to access your list readily and at multiple times each day.

When we internalize something, we believe it, trust it, and live in close relationship to it. It shapes our experiences because of the place it holds inside us. By virtue of being "in" us, it makes claims on us and how we live.

See Allan Hugh Cole Jr., *Good Mourning: Getting through Your Grief* (Louisville, KY: Westminster John Knox Press, 2008), 86.

Incorporate your list frequently in your prayer time. In addition, consider reading over your list as part of your prayer time during the day—so that you read over it at least three times each day (and more is just fine). More will be said about this "three times a day" approach in the next chapter. By following this practice of incorporating your list of Scriptures in your prayer time, you (and others you pray with) will encounter these Scriptures regularly, and with intention, attention, and reflection. Moreover, if others with whom you pray have their own lists, you will be exposed to a wider array of Scripture passages, and so will they, as you share them with one another.

Consider that if you memorize even one passage of Scripture a week, you will know at least fifty in a year, and a hundred in two years, and so on. You may not know them word for word in every case, and that's OK, but you will at least have a deeper sense of what the Bible says, promises, urges, and offers as you pray and live as a follower of Jesus. In other words, you'll know the Christian story more deeply—it will be "in your bones" and will continue to bear much spiritual fruit.

CONTEMPLATIVE PRAYER

The psalmist writes, "Be still before the LORD, and wait patiently for him" (Ps. 37:7). Contemplative prayer may help you with this stillness. Many of us would benefit from more stillness in our lives, especially stillness before God. Not only does stillness foster patience, but according to the psalmist stillness before God and knowledge of God go hand in hand: "Be still, and know that I am God!" (Ps. 46:10). As we become more still before God, we come to know God better, and we await God's presence and guidance more patiently. All of this allows us to deepen our relationship with God, to enjoy "God's benefits," and to bear spiritual fruit. Any type of prayer may foster this stillness, knowledge, and patience, but contemplative prayer proves particularly helpful for some people. It can especially help when life seems to do anything but stand still and patience ranks low on the list of spiritual fruit that we bear.

Webster's Ninth New Collegiate Dictionary defines *contemplate* as follows: "to view or consider with continued attention: meditate on." The dictionary defines *contemplation* as a "concentration on spiritual things as a form of private devotion"; "a state of mystical awareness of God's being"; and "an act of considering with attention: study" or "the act of regarding steadily."[13] We can think of contemplative prayer, then, as a form of praying in which we ponder and give steady and close attention to God and to our lives in relationship to God, while seeking at the same time to keep anything extraneous to these out of awareness. To put it another way, contemplative prayer involves quiet reflection on God and God's leading, such that we assume a posture of devotion as we seek greater awareness of God's being.

Contemplative prayer can take numerous forms. I'll suggest two forms to try: open prayer and centering prayer.

Open Prayer

Open prayer involves the singular goal of opening oneself to God. One can approach the act of opening in different ways. One way is to try not to think about anything and simply let your thoughts be guided by the Spirit. The Quakers practice this type of approach in prayer and in the rest of worship. They get themselves "quiet" before God and await the Spirit's leading. In such a state of quiet openness, you free yourself up from setting any sort of agenda for prayer other than opening yourself entirely to God, such that you make receiving God, experiencing God's presence, and following God's lead your singular object of concentration.

It's difficult for someone to coach you on learning this form of prayer, and you'll likely find that you simply must try it, and probably multiple times, to get the hang of it. It essentially involves letting go of whatever has your attention, interest, and even affection at the moment you pray. In open prayer, you really don't even want to try to think specifically about God, but rather to open yourself to God and allow the Spirit to take it from there. Centering prayer, which we will consider next, involves a more active focus on God than open prayer, which involves freeing or clearing your thinking and feeling to the extent that you can so that the Spirit takes you where it will.

Here are a few suggestions that might help you learn how to pray in this way. One has to do with physical matters. Since opening yourself up to God in this form of prayer remains central, it may help you to incorporate your body in this way of praying. For example, you might sit or stand with your arms extended outward, which results in both a posture of giving and receiving.

In open prayer, we really do seek to give to God whatever prevents our full openness, and so we extend our arms and, perhaps with palms in the air, indicate our desire. At the same time, this posture indicates a desire to receive from God, fully and unencumbered by our own agenda, whatever God would impart. A variation on this approach involves sitting with your palms up in the air while also extending your arms or letting them rest on your knees or in your lap. Think of it this way. These physical postures of openness invite you to rely on the Spirit, and nothing more, to take from you and give to you as God desires. With openness comes deeper trust and reliance on God, which the Scriptures urge for God's people:

> Blessed are those who trust in the LORD,
> whose trust is the LORD.
>
> Jeremiah 17:7

> Trust in the LORD with all your heart,
> and do not rely on your own insight.
>
> Proverbs 3:5

Open Prayer:
Find a comfortable position.
Signal your openness to God with your mind and body.
Wait and trust.
Keep breathing.
Just enjoy *being* together with God!

Here's another posture to consider. In the Roman Catholic tradition, those ordained to the priesthood often incorporate a practice of lying prostrate on the ground (facing down). This practice symbolizes adoration of and submission to God. At the same time, this prostrate position makes for a physical representation of what we seek inwardly and spiritually in prayer, namely, to be in God's presence in the most inviting, welcoming, receptive, and open way. A variation on this practice involves lying prostrate with feet together and arms extended by one's side, which results in the body forming a cross. As the cross is the central symbol of the Christian story, allowing your body to assume its likeness can prove profoundly powerful for your life of prayer and your life of faith.

For some people, it will feel uncomfortable and perhaps even a bit silly to pray in these less common (even odd) bodily positions. If you feel this way, then there's no obligation to try them. However, you might be surprised at how much of an effect your physical position or posture in prayer can have on your experiences of praying. Since the church's inception, followers of Jesus have engaged in these kinds of "physical" prayers with the goal of meeting God in fresh and powerful ways. Praying with attention to your physical posture also reminds you of the answer to the first question posed by the Heidelberg Catechism, a principal confessional document of the Presbyterian and Reformed Christian traditions. The question is "What is your only comfort in life and death?" The answer (in part) is "That I with body and soul, both in life and death, am not my own, but belong unto my faithful savior Jesus Christ." So, why not consider giving some of these practices a try yourself? And, of course, if you find any of them meaningful, feel free to incorporate them (and adapt them) as you pray the Lord's Prayer, pray Scripture, or pray in other ways.

Centering Prayer

Another form of contemplative prayer is called centering prayer.[14] The Roman Catholic tradition has given us this form, more recently made popular by Father Thomas Keating, but people from a wide variety of Christian traditions and individuals who embrace a diversity of theological and religious persuasions now practice it.[15] As its name suggests, it helps center you in relation to God by enhancing your focus on God and God's presence. It shares qualities with open prayer, but whereas in that form you seek to free yourself from attention to anything at all—so that you may be opened fully to the Spirit's work—in centering prayer you focus intently on God and God's presence and leading in your life. You seek "centeredness" in God. This form of contemplative prayer involves honing your focus, whereas open prayer entails letting go of it.

Keating's method for centering prayer involves three steps or movements. First, get yourself still, comfortable, and otherwise prepared to pray. This preparation will likely involve closing your eyes and could further entail some of the suggestions for preparing to pray that we've already considered. Second, begin to let go of all of your thoughts by focusing on just one thought that relates to God. You can do this by focusing your attention on one sacred word. It could be "God," "Jesus," "Christ," or "Holy Spirit," or it could be a word that touches on an attribute of God or the promises of God in the gospel. Whatever sacred word you choose, it will become the focus of your centering approach.

Here are some words to try in centering prayer:

God	Forgiveness
Jesus	Mercy
Christ	Hope
Holy Spirit	Joy
Love	Justice
Peace	Guidance
Grace	

A third step or movement involves allowing the word (and its meaning) to enter fully into your consciousness and your imagination, to become "front and center" in your mind's eye, and then allowing it to remain there as you pray. Keating describes the process as follows: "Introduce the sacred word into your imagination as gently as if you were laying a feather on a piece of absorbent cotton," which suggests welcoming whatever word you settle on into yourself (to internalize it) while not forcing it or holding on to it too tightly. Remember, the word is just that, a word, and it's not the object of your praying. God remains the sole object, which means that if the word begins to "flee" or if other words push into your awareness, either simply recall the sacred word and try again to think of its presence as similar to laying a feather to cotton, or if it seems more helpful, move on to another word and begin the process again.

Deliberate breathing may prove particularly important with both of these contemplative approaches to prayer. So remember to give attention to some type of focused or deliberative breathing. Once again, the spirit of the law should trump the letter as concerns any approach to prayer that you use. Your goal remains the contemplation of God, God's presence, and how God leads you to follow Jesus.

LITURGICAL PRAYER

The last approach to prayer that I will mention is liturgical prayer, or what is sometimes thought of as "worshipful" prayer. The term *liturgy*, from which *liturgical* comes, means "work of the people." Therefore, any type of worship or prayer activity that involves participation of "the people"—whether a congregation or a smaller group gathered together—can rightly be called *liturgical*. However, I'll use this term more narrowly when talking about prayer, such that while liturgical prayer surely involves the participation (work) of those worshiping and praying (whether by themselves or with others), it entails participating in *particular* ways. Specifically, liturgical prayer involves using set prayers and fixed patterns of praying that we typically find in prayer books, worship books, or various devotional guides.

A well-known prayer book is the Episcopal Church's *Book of Common Prayer*. Many so-called liturgical traditions and denominations (e.g., Roman Catholics, Orthodox Christians, Episcopalians, Lutherans, and some strands of United Methodists and Presbyterians) make books like this one central to their worship and prayer practices. These traditions appeal mostly, but for the most part not exclusively, to prayer books and related materials to guide their liturgical life, particularly for public worship but for other occasions as well. Other so-called nonliturgical traditions (e.g., Baptists, the African Methodist Episcopal Church, Congregationalists, Mennonites, Quakers, Pentecostals, and nondenominational or "free church" congregations) use the resources of prayer books and related materials less often if at all. Nevertheless, whether devotees of more liturgical traditions or not, many people who begin a practice of liturgical prayer find it enriching for their prayer lives and for their faith.

So why should you consider making this approach part of your prayer regimen? Because whether in solitary or communal prayer, great benefits can follow from your praying on a consistent basis using *familiar* words and patterns. Early Christianity inherited this practice from ancient Judaism, which made regular use of fixed forms not only in prayers but also for entire worship services. Subsequently, throughout the church's history, similar liturgical practices have been maintained by the majority of Christians worldwide. Having observed their long-standing value for the life of faith, many contemporary Christians continue to use these practices. Here I want to point out several things pertaining to this approach that make it so fruitful and to say why I think that you do well to include it as you exercise your faith in prayer.

First, however, consider that you likely already incorporate liturgical prayer and other practices in your prayer life and in your acts of worship, whether you belong to a liturgical tradition or not. After all, when praying the Lord's Prayer and praying Scripture, when following an order of worship on Sunday morning, or when singing hymns that you know and have sung before, you make use of familiar words and patterns. Your "work" of praying or worshiping incorporates these. The same holds true when you recite the great ecumenical creeds, like the Apostles' Creed and the Nicene Creed, which numerous Christian traditions embrace and include in their regular services of worship and prayers. In each of these cases, you appeal to well-known, time-tested, and widely embraced words and fixed forms of expressing yourself before God, many of which have held special meaning and importance for a great number of people who have followed Jesus for thousands of years.

But you need not limit yourself to these sources of liturgical prayer and worship, as significant as they remain. You can draw from additional liturgical aids to help exercise your faith. These may include official prayer books that various denominations publish and use, but they may also include collections of prayers, devotional guides, and similar resources.

> Try praying the Apostles' Creed:
> I believe in God the Father Almighty, Maker of heaven and earth.
> I believe in Jesus Christ God's only son, our Lord; who was conceived by the Holy Spirit, born of the Virgin Mary, suffered under Pontius Pilate, was crucified, dead, and buried; he descended into hell; the third day he rose again from the dead; he ascended into heaven, and sitteth at the right hand of God the Father Almighty; from thence he shall come to judge the quick and the dead.
> I believe in the Holy Spirit; the holy catholic church; the communion of saints; the forgiveness of sins; the resurrection of the body; and the life everlasting. Amen.

Note that much of the value of using these liturgical aids lies in the familiarity that one acquires with them over time. Take, for example, the Presbyterian Church (U.S.A.)'s *Book of Common Worship*, which lists numerous prayers and also provides patterns for prayer and worship for use in a variety of settings. As you pray these prayers and make use of these patterns regularly, you become more accustomed to them. Eventually, you may learn them by heart, such that they become familiar and possibly even sacred companions that you regularly invite into your time with God in prayer. Moreover, with familiarity comes *internalization*—having the well-known prayers and patterns become a deep part of you so that you have them "in your bones." This internalization allows you at any time to make an appeal to and even rely on carefully chosen words and patterns that you have prayed before and that many others have prayed, found meaningful, and relied on themselves, in some cases for centuries.

WHY PRAY THIS WAY?

Why does internalizing the words of well-known prayers matter? Because there will almost certainly be times in your life when you do not have the words to pray, hard as you may try to find them and want to find them. The same holds true for most of us. For many people, the dearth of words comes during the particularly painful times of their lives. Painful experiences often bring disorientation and fatigue, which can result in your being "speechless," perhaps especially before God. You hear people indicate this when they say things like "There are no words," or "I just don't know what to say," or "I try to pray and nothing comes out." I've heard these types of experiences conveyed many times, and I've felt similarly myself. I suspect that you have, too.

When we lack the words that we want or need to utter, however, we can rely on others' words to speak for us and on our behalf. It is one significant way that those who follow Jesus may share their lives and look to one another for mutual support. Regardless of whether the words that you rely on have been provided by the "saints" of faith or by us rather "ordinary" followers of Jesus and regardless of whether these words come from Scripture, confessional statements and creeds, or prayer books and similar liturgical aids, praying them can bring great joy, comfort, and hope.

As a matter of fact, you may learn to lean on them, allowing them to prop you up and steady you before God or others when you sense that your own words lack this ability. You may even allow yourself to "fall" into these words that others speak to God on your behalf, so that they surround, protect, or buoy you as you have the need. This practice of looking to others' words to empower your own prayer life may prove especially meaningful and comforting if you recall the *unifying* power of liturgical prayer. Praying what others have prayed (and may very well be praying still, just as you are), allows you to stand with them all—and they with you—in shared acts of addressing God and expecting God's response.

At the same time, remember that liturgical prayer may enrich your life of faith more broadly, such that you may rely on it not merely in times of struggling for your own words or feeling particularly pained or in need, but at any time as part of your ongoing prayer life and growth in your faith. A few years ago, a friend of mine said something that I find helpful to keep in mind when thinking about liturgical acts and their potential value. Perhaps you will find this helpful, too. She was raised in a so-called nonliturgical tradition and had served as one of its pastors for many years. However, she decided to become Lutheran, a tradition that embraces liturgical practices and even places them at the center of the church's shared life. When I asked what prompted her to move so far from her tradition of birth to her newly chosen tradition, she said something that has stuck with me. She said, "I think I found it freeing to realize that neither I nor the people I was trying to serve had to rely so much on *my* words, *my* prayers, or *my* way of conducting worship, but together we could rely on *others'* ways of doing these things, along with our own, in a shared life of faith."

In recounting her experiences I do not mean to suggest that the only or even "best" way to follow Jesus entails strict adherence to a liturgical tradition. Some who follow Jesus will want to incorporate more liturgical acts; others will use liturgical prayer less often. My friend would fully agree. However, incorporating liturgical practices in your prayer life may indeed prove freeing in ways similar to what my friend experienced. So I am advocating that you consider it as one approach that may help you grow in prayer and faith, regardless of whether you also address God using your own words, which I assume you will continue to do. After all, both ways of addressing God have their place in a prayerful life. Moreover, although the other three approaches to prayer may hold a more central place in your prayer life (i.e., using the Lord's Prayer, praying Scripture, and engaging in contemplative prayer), both now and in the future, liturgical prayer can provide a rich supplement to these other forms. Additionally, on a very practical level, praying with a prayer book or something similar lends itself to praying with others as well as praying in solitude.

SUGGESTIONS FOR PRAYING LITURGICALLY

Here are a few basic suggestions for adding liturgical prayer to your prayer life, including when you pray by yourself and when you pray with others.

Find a resource that speaks to you and stick with it. Perhaps a prayer book or worship book from your tradition will be the best place to begin. Or if you prefer, consider perusing the bookshelves of your church library, a local bookstore, or looking online for a "guide to prayer," a "devotional guide," or something similar. Here are a few that I think are well worth consideration:

I Want to Live These Days with You: A Year of Daily Devotions, by Dietrich Bonhoeffer (Louisville, KY: Westminster John Knox Press, 2007).

Healing Liturgies for the Seasons of Life, by Abigail Rian Evans (Louisville, KY: Westminster John Knox Press, 2004).

Praying with Beads: Daily Prayers for the Christian Year, by Nan Lewis Doerr and Virginia Stem Owens (Grand Rapids: Wm. B. Eerdmans Publishing Co., 2007).

Making Time for God: Daily Devotions for Children and Families to Share, by Susan R. Garrett and Amy Plantinga Pauw (Grand Rapids: Baker Books, 2002).

Celtic Treasures: Daily Scriptures and Prayer, by J. Philip Newell (Grand Rapids: Wm. B. Eerdmans Publishing Co., 2005).

A Guide to Prayer for All Who Seek God, by Norman Shawchuck and Reuben P. Job (Nashville: Upper Room Books, 2006).

The Only Necessary Thing: Living a Prayerful Life, by Henri J. M. Nouwen, ed. Wendy Wilson Greer (New York: Crossroad Publishing Co., 1999).

The Westminster Collection of Christian Prayers, ed. Dorothy M. Stewart (Louisville, KY: Westminster John Knox Press, 2002).

When you settle on a resource to help guide you in your prayer life, commit to using it for at least a week, and for longer if possible. I suggest this amount of time because it usually takes a while to become familiar enough with a new liturgical aid to gauge whether it's right for you. In my experience, while you will appreciate some of these resources more than others, most well-chosen ones can provide something that will speak to you and help you grow. Some of the guides that I have suggested call for a more lengthy engagement, including up to a year or more. Of course, if you begin with any book and discern that it's not right for you, then to move to another. On the other hand, if you find a gem that you can spend a lengthy amount of time with, be sure to make the most of it.

Include the resource in at least one of your acts of praying each day. If you follow the three-times-a-day approach that I detail in the next chapter—or if you pray more often—consider making liturgical prayer a central part of at least one of those times. For example, you might want to make praying the Lord's Prayer the focus in the morning, give attention to praying Scripture in the afternoon, and then practice a form of liturgical prayer in the evening. Or maybe you'll prefer this plan: contemplative prayer in the morning, liturgical prayer at noon, and praying Scripture at night. Again, you'll know best what seems right for you.

Involve at least one additional person in your acts of liturgical prayer at least one time each week. As we have noted, a faithful and growth-filled life of prayer will involve praying in solitude and praying with other people. Many people who make use of liturgical prayer note its particular power for encouraging and sustaining prayer with others, especially that which takes place beyond a formal worship service. Moreover, those who feel bashful or intimidated by the prospects of praying with others while using their own words sometimes find it easier to draw on other words that prayer books or similar liturgical aids provide. So consider finding one or more people who will share in a regular practice of liturgical prayer with you at least one time a week (and more often is just fine). It could be that once you have your partner or partners on board, you can decide together what your plans for praying will involve and what resources or aids you will try.

Allow yourself to be "stretched." Praying with others tends to provide opportunities for hearing different perspectives, encountering alternative styles and emphases, and trying new approaches to the chief exercise of faith. All of these experiences can serve to challenge you in fresh ways, to beckon you to stretch beyond your comfort zones, and to help you grow. With this likelihood in mind, give some thought both to the persons and aids that might stretch you most appropriately. You might want to pray with a person older or younger than yourself. Perhaps you'll want to pray with persons of the opposite gender, or from different racial or ethnic backgrounds. Maybe you'll be stretched by praying with someone from another religious tradition, or someone who holds a different theological persuasion than you do. Perhaps you find liturgical approaches to prayer and worship problematic or hold these in suspicion. If so, it could be that praying with someone who feels more at home in a liturgical tradition will enrich your prayer life. Or maybe you identify more with the "head" than with the "heart" when it comes to your faith, and partnering with someone who leads more with the heart than you do will foster growth. You will have to decide whether and to what extent you want and need "stretching." You'll also know best how to partner with persons to help foster this. Just remember to commit to discovering these things, keeping in mind that praying with people and with approaches that expand your own experiences and proclivities can prove invaluable.

A PRAYER FOR YOU TO PRAY

(Prepare yourself to pray by getting yourself still, taking a few breaths, and opening yourself up to God.)

> O LORD, our Sovereign,
>> how majestic is your name in all the earth!
>>>> Psalm 8:9

You know our thoughts before we think them, O God; and before we speak you know what we will say. And yet you still call us to "pray without ceasing" so that we might live as prayerful people. Not only this, but you also provide so many ways of praying, and all we need to do is to try them. Help me and all of those who seek you in prayer to do so with energy, commitment, passion, and trust. And as we enjoy the privilege of prayer, may we never take it for granted or overlook its significance for faith. These things I pray in the name of Jesus Christ. Amen.

Chapter 6

HOW DO WE KEEP PRAYING?

Rejoice always; pray without ceasing.
1 Thessalonians 5:16–17

Having considered different ways of praying, let's now think about how to *keep* praying once you begin. In other words, let's consider how you can make praying a regular part of your daily life, such that it becomes second nature.

"Lord, teach us to pray" (Luke 11:1). This request came from one of his disciples after Jesus had finished praying. The disciple recognized, as Bonhoeffer put it, that "we must *learn* to pray."[1] We are not born knowing how, nor do we become capable of praying automatically. Instead, we must be taught to pray; we must be instructed in how to do it. Instruction can come from various sources, including the Bible and church traditions, books like this one, and observations of what others say about prayer and how they practice it, such as a minister or other person in a congregation. All of these may provide you with essential instruction for learning how to pray.

YOU LEARN TO PRAY BY PRAYING

It is important for you to learn how to pray from different sources, but for true learning to occur, something else must happen. You also have to put the instruction that you receive into practice. *Experience* is the best teacher. You learn best how to pray by experiencing prayer—that is, by praying. Nothing substitutes for this. Jesus confirmed as much by telling the disciples, "'When you pray, say . . .'" (Luke 11:2). Notice that Jesus didn't say, "Think about prayer in this way" or "In order to learn how to pray, learn these concepts and ponder these things." Nor did Jesus say, "Just watch me pray if you want to learn how," although the disciples could have learned something from watching Jesus and Jesus had just been praying when the disciple, who presumably *was* watching, put the question of how to pray before Jesus. Rather, Jesus essentially said, "You will learn to pray by doing it, and here's how." He pointed to the necessity of experiencing prayer and practicing at it.

With Jesus' response in mind, I suggest that building a more deliberate, faithful, and rewarding prayer life requires that you pray persistently. Prayer has to become a central activity of your life, a practice that finds a deeply valued place in your daily routine. To put it another way, prayer has to become for you a principal focus and a core interest from which others spring. This requires that you dedicate a good deal of intention, attention, and reflection to prayer; but you also must engage in a persistent *practice* of this "chief exercise of faith." This chapter seeks to provide some help.

Perhaps you find yourself struggling to establish a practice of persistent prayer—we could call it a prayer regimen—and you feel discouraged about these challenges. Or maybe you feel pretty satisfied with your prayer life, but you still want to enrich it and grow in your faith. Perhaps you would describe your experience with prayer as falling somewhere between "struggle" and "satisfaction," but you have curiosity about how to pray differently and want to explore this interest. Either way, prayer can become a more central part of your life and help to deepen your faith.

The best prayer regimen will likely involve each of these four approaches that we considered in the previous chapter, though you should feel free to practice them in ways that feel most helpful and meaningful to you. None of these methods should be viewed or practiced inflexibly, nor should anyone approach prayer as if "one size fits all." I encourage you to make use of these approaches in ways that best fit you, taking into consideration your own faith tradition, beliefs, needs, and preferences, and most important, your sense of God's leading. I should add that whatever approach you choose, you will learn to pray most faithfully by looking to Jesus as you pray. In fact, we can and should observe how Jesus prayed and heed his instructions on prayer, along with learning from other examples of prayer found in the Scriptures. We look to Jesus and these other sources for guidance, with the understanding that we must take what they teach us and put it into practice for true learning to occur. Spending time reading the Bible's accounts of prayer and allowing them to serve as models for your own prayer life yields good results—spiritual fruit. So, plan on incorporating this practice into your prayer life.

> Find a regular pattern of prayer, something that works for you!

Whatever your approach, I urge you to keep two additional things in mind. First, the Christian story remains the central focus and basis for your own story, and it thus remains the focus and basis for your praying. Second, remember to practice these approaches to prayer not simply by yourself but also with others who seek to follow Jesus and to exercise their faith. As you will likely discover, acts of solitary prayer that arise from acts of praying in community and then feed back into them will prove most instructive and teach you how to pray as you want.

MAKING A HABIT OF PRAYER

Let's think about how to establish and maintain a disciplined *practice* of prayer—an exercise regimen for a prayerful life. Many people who find prayer a challenge admit that they only pray occasionally, perhaps when they feel particularly troubled by something or when it occurs to them that praying could prove helpful in some way. When serving as a pastor, I remember visiting my friend Joe in the hospital before a major surgery and his saying to me, "I never prayed much before finding out I had to do this, but I've made up for it since then!" On another occasion, someone facing the loss of a job remarked, "I better get going with my prayers. The clock is ticking, and I'm going to need all the help I can get." I've heard these kinds of remarks on other occasions, too. To tell the truth, I've thought similar things myself, even if I didn't say it. Whatever the circumstances, finding ourselves in need of aid, reassurance, or hope tends to bring us to our knees most quickly and decisively. Maybe your experience has been like this, too.

Note that praying every now and then, although better than not praying at all, will not yield the kind of growth in your prayer life or in your faith that comes with praying consistently and in a more disciplined way. The richest and most rewarding prayer life will be one marked by regular acts of prayer, up to several times a day, perhaps, regardless of what's going on in your life or whether you feel troubled or not. Of course, we certainly can and should continue to pray when we feel the need, like when facing some difficulty and wanting assurance and support from God.

> I call upon God,
> and the LORD will save me.
> Psalm 55:16

But we should not make times of difficulty and need for support the *only* occasions for prayer. Nor should prayer become a kind of afterthought that occurs only occasionally and in unpredictable ways. Instead, prayer should remain at the front of our minds—a forethought for daily living. The apostle Paul seems to have recognized the value of this latter approach when he urged that we "pray without ceasing" (1 Thess. 5:17). In other words, prayer should inform all that we do, with each waking moment lived in a "posture" of praying. Like most things in life that we want to improve, enrich, or advance, building a life of prayer calls for rigorous and regular energy and focus.

We do well, therefore, to think about making prayer into what we could call a "life pattern" or a *habit*.[2] Praying needs to become something so central to how we think, feel, act, relate, and live that it becomes second nature. Praying must become a necessary life practice, such that if we don't do it, we feel its absence in a profound way. You hear people who engage in regular physical exercise say something similar when they miss a few days in their routine. They say things like "I just don't feel like myself," or "I missed my workout and it shows," or "I have to get back into my rhythm." Their physical activity has become so much a part of their lives and contributes so significantly to their sense of well-being that they notice its absence and feel eager to reclaim it. We could say that in these cases their exercise regimen has become habitual.

> Sometimes it helps to think of prayer as a habit—or as a rhythm that keeps life going.

In the late nineteenth century, philosopher and psychologist William James pointed out that our lives basically operate according to "laws of habit." Putting forth a "psychology of habituation," he claimed that "all of our life, so far as it has definite form, is but a mass of habits—practical, emotional, and intellectual—systematically organized for our weal or woe, and bearing us irresistibly towards our destiny, whatever the latter may be."[3] For James, almost all of what we do in life comes "second nature" because it follows from habits that we have in place.

> Ninety-nine hundredths or, possibly, nine hundred and ninety-nine thousandths of our activity is purely automatic and habitual, . . . things of a type so fixed by repetition as almost to be classed as reflex actions.
>
> William James, *Talks to Teachers on Psychology; and to Students on Some of Life's Ideals* (New York: Literary Classics of the United States, 1987), 751.

I suspect that you can identify to some degree with James's claims. Most of us probably can. For the most part we do live quite habitually, perhaps more than we recognize. Whether our habits have to do with our faith commitments, our political persuasions, the way we experience conflict or problem solve, how we spend money, or the kind of people we tend to seek out and spend time with; whether they involve the time we get up in the morning and go to bed at night, the various rituals or routines we engage in to get ready for work or school or when we return home from these; or whether our habits have to do with what we eat, where we sit in church, how we manage time, where we vacation, where we purchase certain things that we need, or many other facets of our lives—we tend to approach these things in pretty much the same way. We think, feel, and act according to patterns put in place by previous experiences, patterns that become habitually maintained. Some of us operate more habitually than others do, and we are each more habitual about certain things and less so about other things. But most of us live according to the laws of habit that James identified. Many people even refer to themselves as "creatures of habit," pointing to the fact that what they think and feel, and especially how they act, happens more or less automatically and with regularity and consistency.

James also recognized that habits can and do change. Although operative habits play a powerful role in our daily lives, we have the ability to break them and form different ones. We may also strengthen or enrich habits that seem especially beneficial or healthy. How can this happen? Through a process of learning more and more about our current habits and how they influence us, we can decide which ones we wish to maintain and what new ones we'd like to form, and we can change how we act, feel, and think accordingly. In other words, if we approach our habits more consciously and conscientiously—with intention, attention, and reflection, and with an eye toward whether or not we want to keep embracing them— we have the ability to change them. In James's words, we can alter the "practical, emotional, and intellectual" aspects of our lives.

Faithful prayer takes on the qualities of a habit. As with most habits, approaching prayer with more intention, attention, and reflection results in your doing it more often. The more you do it, the richer the practice can grow and the more it can become simply part of what you always do, something that holds a key place in your life that you crave in its absence. Consequently, you feel more "fit," energized, and passionate about what you're doing, which serves to make you want to do it even more. In other words, your habit of praying becomes even more habitual. This does not mean that you always have to pray the same way. In chapter 5 I discussed four different ways to pray while also reminding you that plenty of other ways may also prove helpful and even essential for a more prayerful life. So I urge you to try lots of different ways of praying. Nevertheless, making use of these four ways to pray, while also keeping in mind the goal of making them elements of a life habit of praying, should help you exercise your faith in more beneficial and meaningful ways. The sections that follow provide suggestions for how you might develop a habitual life pattern of faithful prayer.

FREQUENCY AND RHYTHMS OF PRAYING

I suggest beginning with a commitment to praying three times a day for at least five minutes each time. In addition, consider praying before meals, too, even if briefly. This practice serves not only to remind you of God's provision of "daily bread," but it can also keep you mindful of your praying rhythm while also complementing the prayers that you offer at other times. I also suggest praying with at least one other person, and more is usually better, one or more times each week beyond what you do in a weekly worship service at church. This sort of practice will ensure that you engage regularly in both solitary and communal prayer, the virtues of which have been noted.

A natural rhythm for many people involves praying shortly after waking in the morning, praying again at lunchtime or in the early afternoon, and then praying again in the evening, perhaps just before retiring to bed. Maybe these times of day will work well for you, too. If not, try other times, but commit to praying at least three times each day. Also try to pray for a minimum of five minutes each time you pray. For some, this amount of time will seem paltry, and they'll want to pray longer. Great! I encourage this. Perhaps beginning with ten minutes, or even fifteen, will prove the better approach. You'll have a sense of what works best for you, but keep in mind that you want to be challenged but not overwhelmed as you implement (or enhance) your prayer regimen. However, for many people, and especially those who have not prayed before with much regularity, five minutes will seem challenging enough. When you feel as though praying three times a day for at least a five- (or ten- or fifteen-) minute stretch has become an established regimen that seems to bear spiritual fruit for you, feel free to increase the frequency. And if you have more time some days than other days, or more time, say, in the evening than in the morning, use the time that you have to pray as best you can, and don't worry about it. The goal remains simply to pray regularly, not to log a specific amount of prayer time per se.

PLACES AND POSTURES FOR PRAYING

Try praying in varied places and in different physical positions or postures. It might surprise you how much this approach can help keep your prayer life fresh and interesting. Here are some examples. Try praying routinely in a church sanctuary if you have access, whether by yourself or with others—and, again, I have in mind additional times beyond set worship services. The church is where the faith community gathers on a regular basis to worship, pray, serve, and live as Jesus' followers. Jesus also refers to the place where the community gathers as "a house of prayer," which suggests that frequent acts of praying should take place there (Mark 11:17). But you can feel free to pray in other settings, too.

Consider finding a spot or two outdoors, in places that provide you with a sense of peace, beauty, and God's creative work. Furthermore, most of us like to have a spot in our homes where we tend to pray, perhaps an out-of-the-way place that invites quiet reflection and communion with God. So consider having three or four places where you pray regularly. You don't want too many, since it's important to have designated places to return to regularly in order to pray. In fact, many people say that they benefit from having a sense that "these are my places of prayer" and from visiting them as a matter of routine, as opposed to simply going to a different place every time they pray.

You can pray at church, at home, outdoors, or somewhere else.

As for physical postures, try praying on your knees if your health and flexibility allow it. Literally falling to one's knees before God can prove quite powerful. This practice is highly regarded in the Scriptures, evidenced by Paul saying,

For it is written,
"As I live, says the Lord, every knee shall bow to me,
and every tongue shall give praise to God."
Romans 14:11

In his letter to the Ephesians, Paul also writes, "I bow my knees before the Father, from whom every family in heaven and on earth takes its name" (Eph. 3:14).

You also might find it rewarding to pray with your arms extended and your palms upward, since this literally opens you up to God and conveys expectancy in prayer. Or perhaps you'd rather place your hands together, a practice many of us learned as children, and bow your head to pray. Another good prayer posture involves sitting in a chair or on a bench with your back straight, your feet flat on the floor, and your hands resting on your knees (whether palms are facing downward or upward).

There's a wonderful practice in traditional Judaism that you might want to try. It involves simply rocking back and forth, slowly but deliberately, using a slight bowing motion, while reciting fixed prayers over and over again (an act called *davening*, meaning "to pray," in Yiddish). Those who practice davening say that it fosters focus and concentration and that it sharpens their attention to praying. It's not required in Judaism, and you need not feel obligated to try it, but consider doing so to see if it's helpful. Or perhaps you'd rather just sit in a comfortable chair to pray. This is fine, too. But I urge you not to make it too comfortable because sitting too comfortably often leads to feeling sleepy. You want to pray in a way that fosters concentration and alertness, not slumber!

You also may want to try praying as you look at some religious symbol that's meaningful to you, such as a cross, a Bible, a baptismal font, a communion table, or even a piece of art that reminds you of the Christian story and your place in it. Try holding some of these in your hands while you pray, such as a cross or Bible, or maybe touching the water in the font, as these practices prove significant for many people. These efforts foster a praying experience that includes not just your mind or spirit but your body as well.

> You can pray standing, sitting, or kneeling—or many other ways.

Remember that no matter what specific things you incorporate in your prayer life, you should feel free to change them sometimes, too. Again, there's no one or two or even three set ways to pray. There are many ways to pray, and variety usually provides the richest kind of prayer life.

PREPARING TO PRAY

Whatever your methods, frequency, and rhythms of praying, I also recommend *preparing* yourself for prayer each time you do it. You might think of this preparation in terms of warming up to exercise your faith. This, too, will mean different things to different people, but you promote intention, attention, and reflection in prayer by readying yourself for praying. For many of you, it will involve finding a quiet place (whether when alone or with others), perhaps sitting still for a few moments, and maybe closing your eyes and taking a deep breath or two in order to relax. You might even want to say (or pray) something along these lines: "Gracious God, I seek your presence in prayer. Help me prepare myself for this privilege"; "Dear God, please help me get myself ready to pray"; or "I find it difficult to pray just now, so please help me, O God." Asking God to help you focus can be a wonderfully rewarding way to prepare you for the act of praying.

> Try beginning your prayer with one of these verses:
> "Be still, and know that I am God!" (Ps. 46:10)
> "Be still before the LORD, and wait patiently for him."
> (Ps. 37:7)

Remember, too, that breathing in particular ways can help to still you and to give you focus. You might prepare to pray by taking several slow but deep breaths, and then breathing out in a similarly slow but deliberate manner.

Some people will want to spend several minutes engaging
in nothing but deliberate (prayerful) breathing, for this has
positive effects on one's physical, mental, emotional, and
even spiritual states. Keep in mind, too, that you can incorporate acts of deliberative breathing in various forms of
prayer, as we discussed in chapter 5.

FINDING A PRAYER PARTNER

I suggest that you seek out at least one person to pray
with regularly—a prayer "partner," if you will. Some may
think of this as rather hokey or as something that feels
contrived if not foreign. Others may associate having a
prayer partner exclusively with so-called "conservative"
or "evangelical" Christians, with whom they might not
identify so closely if at all. Moreover, for those who think
of faith and prayer as essentially private matters, enlisting
another (or others) to pray with oneself regularly may
prove challenging.

But there may be great value in this practice for you.
Consider that many people have exercise partners, reading
partners (book clubs, for example), fishing partners, sewing
partners, dance partners, cooking partners, and partners for
many other activities that they engage in. Partners not only
enrich our experiences with these activities, allowing for the
pleasure that comes with sharing something that we enjoy
with others who enjoy it too; partners can also keep us
accountable, focused, and "on track" as we engage in these
pursuits. Many people who enjoy running or working out at
a gym, for example, say that they need a partner to help
motivate them sometimes, like when they need a push to get
out of bed on those more difficult mornings and head to the

track or gym. Many of the same people report that checking in with someone regularly to share progress (or regression) serves to keep them attuned to what they are doing or what they might need to do in order to meet their goals. We might even say that our partners help us deepen and maintain our efforts toward intention, attention, and reflection regarding our shared interests and activities. So I encourage you to think about how you will invite someone, or several persons, to partner with you in this chief exercise of faith.

A PROGRAM FOR EXERCISING YOUR FAITH

I've tried to stress the fact that you will need to figure out what sort of prayer and prayer regimen best suit you and your needs. Nevertheless, some people find it useful to have a suggested program for helping them establish their own routines of praying. With this in mind, I offer the following programs for exercising your faith in prayer. Remember that these are very basic, and you should feel free to adapt them however you wish. Also, don't feel the need to increase the amount of time that you pray—and thus to move from one program to the next—too quickly. If you're new to praying, it's likely that you'll want to spend several weeks on program 1 before moving to program 2, and so on. If you feel ready, though, don't hesitate to try a new program. You can always revert back to a previous one if you need to.

Program 1

Spend two minutes in prayer three times during the day, totaling six minutes.

A.M.: Pray the Lord's Prayer three times, pausing each time you complete it.

Noon: Pray one Scripture passage three times, pausing between each recitation.

P.M.: Spend two minutes in centering prayer, using the suggested method.

Program 2

Spend five minutes in prayer three times during the day, totaling fifteen minutes.

A.M.: Pray the Lord's Prayer three times, pausing to reflect between each line.

Noon: Pray one Scripture passage three times, pausing to reflect after each recitation.

P.M.: Spend five minutes in either open or centering prayer.

Program 3

Spend ten minutes in prayer three times during the day, totaling thirty minutes.

A.M.: Spend ten minutes in open or centering prayer.

Noon: Pray two or three Scriptures several times, pausing to reflect after each recitation.

P.M.: Spend ten minutes in liturgical prayer with a resource of your choosing.

Program 4

Spend fifteen minutes in prayer three times during the day, totaling forty-five minutes.

A.M.: Pray one to three Scriptures several times, pausing to reflect after each recitation.

Noon: Spend fifteen minutes in liturgical prayer with a resource of your choosing.

P.M.: Pray the Lord's Prayer five times, pausing to reflect after each recitation.

Program 5

Spend twenty minutes in prayer three times during the day, totaling one hour.

A.M.: Pray one to three Scriptures multiple times, pausing to reflect after each recitation; or pray the Lord's Prayer five to seven times, pausing to reflect between each line.

Noon: Spend twenty minutes in liturgical prayer with a resource of your choosing.

P.M.: Spend twenty minutes in either open or centering prayer.

POSTSCRIPT

Prayer is one of God's greatest gifts. In prayer, we can approach God, grow in relationship to God, deepen our faith, and live more and more as the people God has created and called us to be. This is why Paul urged that we "pray without ceasing" (1 Thess. 5:17). Nevertheless, praying does not come easily or effortlessly for everyone. In fact, most people will find prayer challenging to some extent, even after they become "proficient" at it and even after they have established a regular prayer routine. When you struggle with prayer, remember that those who knew Jesus most personally, his first disciples, needed him to teach them how to pray. Recall, too, that the apostle Paul noted the struggles that many who follow Jesus have with prayer but also the Spirit's aid: "The Spirit helps us in our weakness; for we do not know how to pray as we ought, but that very Spirit intercedes with sighs too deep for words" (Rom. 8:26).

People who want to follow Jesus are called to pray, but doing so usually takes some work on our parts. Perhaps having to work at prayer serves to make it all the more significant and helps us recognize its value more clearly. So keep working at it! Expect that you'll struggle at times, but when you do, lean more and more on God and trust that this will be sufficient. Moreover, when you pray, keep the words of the psalmist in mind:

I call upon you, for you will answer me, O God;
incline your ear to me, hear my words.

Psalm 17:6

Calling on God in prayer and trusting that God will hear
your words will help you exercise your faith.

NOTES

CHAPTER 2: WHY DO WE PRAY?

1. See, for example, 1 Sam. 7:8; 12:23; Neh. 1:6; Jer. 37:3; 42:2–4.

2. See, for example, Matt. 14:23; 26:36; Mark 6:46; 14:35; Luke 5:16; 6:12; 22:41.

3. See, for example, Matt. 6:5–14; 24:20; 26:41; Mark 13:18; 14:38; Luke 11:2; 18:1–8; 22:40.

4. See, for example, Acts 2:42; 8:22, 24; 10:9; 26:29; Rom. 8:26; 1 Cor. 14:15; 2 Cor. 9:14; 13:7, 9; Eph. 1:17; 3:13, 16, 18; 6:18–20; Col. 4:3; 1 Thess. 3:10; 5:17, 25; 2 Thess. 1:11; 3:1; 1 Tim. 2:8; Phlm. 1:6; Heb. 13:18; Jas. 5:13–16; 3 John 1:2; Jude 1:20.

5. John Calvin, *Institutes of the Christian Religion*, ed. John T. McNeill, trans. Ford Lewis Battles, 2 vols. (Philadelphia: Westminster Press, 1960), 1:301.

6. Karl Barth, *Dogmatics in Outline*, trans. G. T. Thomson (New York: Philosophical Library, 1947), 38.

7. This metaphor comes from Frederick W. Schmidt, *When Suffering Persists* (Harrisburg, PA: Morehouse, 2001), 54.

8. Karl Barth, *Prayer*, ed. Don E. Saliers, trans. Sara F. Terrien (Louisville, KY: Westminster John Knox Press, 2002), 13.

9. Barth, *Dogmatics in Outline*, 38–39.

10. See, for example, 1 Sam. 12:23; 1 Thess. 5:17.

11. See, for example, Matt. 14:23; 26:36; Mark 6:46; 14:32; Luke 5:16; 9:28.

12. See, for example, Luke 9:18; 11:1.

13. Barth, *Prayer*, 17–18.

14. See, for example, Gen. 20:17; 25:21; Exod. 8:30; 10:18; Num. 11:2; 21:7; 1 Sam. 1:10, 27; 2:1, 8:6; 2 Sam. 24:10, 17; 2 Kgs. 6:17–18; 19:15; 20:2; 2 Chr. 30:18; 32:20, 24; 33:13; Ezra 10:1; Neh. 2:4; 4:9; Job 42:10; Jer. 32:16; Dan. 9:4; Jonah 2:1; 4:2.

15. See, for example, Matt. 6:5–18, 25–34.

16. Dietrich Bonhoeffer, *Dietrich Bonhoeffer Works*, vol. 4, *Discipleship*, ed. Geffrey B. Kelly and John D. Godsey, trans. Barbara Green and Reinhard Krauss, English ed. (Minneapolis: Fortress Press, 2001), 152–53.

17. Ibid., 152–53.

18. Here I am indebted especially to Bonhoeffer. See ibid., 152–58.

19. I use the term "living Christ" to identify Christian belief in the resurrected Jesus and the ongoing work of the Holy Spirit, which makes Christ present in the life of the believer.

20. See also, for example, Mark 10:32–33; Luke 10:22; 22:9; John 5:36–37; 6:40; 8:16, 18–19, 28, 54; 10:15, 18, 29, 37; 12:49; 14:7, 10, 13, 20, 21, 23–24; 15:9–10, 15–16, 23, 24; 16:23; 17:24; 20:17.

21. See, for example, John 3:35; 5:20; 11:3; 13:34; 15:9, 12.

22. Scriptural warrant for this "priestly" status before God includes Heb. 4:14–16; 6:13–20; 1 Pet. 2:4–10; Rev. 1:4–6; 5:6–10.

23. Bonhoeffer, *Discipleship*, 153.

24. See, for example, Luke 1:79; 2:32; John 1:4–5, 7–9.

25. See Matt. 5:1–7:29 and Luke 6:20–49. Luke has Jesus imparting these teachings on a "plain" as opposed to a "mountain." Hence we typically distinguish between the Sermon on the Mount (Matthew's version) and the Sermon on the Plain (Luke's version), even though these convey essentially the same teachings.

26. See, for example, 2 Sam. 22:4; Ps. 17:6; 18:3; 55:16; 141:1; Isa. 55:6; Jer. 29:12.

27. Calvin likens the failure to pray to missing out on treasure that we could enjoy. See Calvin, *Institutes,* 2:850.

28. Ibid., 2:851.

29. See also Matt. 26:36–46; Luke 22:39–46; Heb. 5:7–8.

30. See, for example, John 14:25–27; Acts 1:8; Rom. 5:5.

31. See Allan Hugh Cole Jr., *Good Mourning: Getting through Your Grief* (Louisville, KY: Westminster John Knox Press, 2008), 85–92.

32. See, for example, Acts 4:31; 5:32; John 14:15–17, 26; 16:13; 20:22; 1 John 3:24; 4:13.

33. See, for example, Gen. 32:10; Exod. 4:10; Matt. 3:11; Mark 1:7; Luke 3:16; John 1:27; 1 Cor. 15:9.

CHAPTER 3: WHAT ARE THE BENEFITS OF PRAYER?

1. Karl Barth, *Prayer*, ed. Don E. Saliers, trans. Sara F. Terrien (Louisville, KY: Westminster John Knox Press, 2002), 14. We should note here, too, that for Barth, when God looks through Christ, he looks at all people.

2. John Calvin, *Institutes of the Christian Religion*, ed. John T. McNeill, trans. Ford Lewis Battles, 2 vols. (Philadelphia: Westminster Press, 1960), 1:5–39.

3. Ibid., 2:850.

4. Barth, *Prayer*, 20–21.

5. See, for example, Acts 2:42; Eph. 1:17; 1 Thess. 5:25; Jas. 5:13–14; Jude 1:20.

6. See, for example, 1 John 3:11, 14, 23; 4:7–11, 12; 2 John 1:5; Eph. 5:2.

7. Robert H. Schuller, *If It's Going to Be, It's Up to Me: Eight Proven Principles of Possibility Thinking* (New York: HarperCollins), 1998.

8. Ibid., 5–6.

9. See, for example, Isa. 58:7; Luke 3:11; John 15:13–15; Acts 2:44; 4:32; 2 Cor. 1:7; 9:8; Gal. 6:2; Eph. 4:28; 6:23; Phil. 1:7; 4:14; 1 Thess. 2:8; 1 Tim. 6:18; 2 Tim. 2:3; Titus 1:4; Heb. 13:16.

10. See, for example, Matt. 4:19; 8:22; 9:9; 10:38; 16:24; 19:21; Mark 1:17; 2:14; 8:34; 10:21; Luke 5:27; 9:23, 59; 14:27; 18:22; John 1:43; 12:26; 13:36; 21:19, 22.

11. Thomas à Kempis, *The Imitation of Christ*, trans. Joseph N. Tylenda (New York: Vintage Books, 1998).

12. Dietrich Bonhoeffer, *Dietrich Bonhoeffer Works*, vol. 4, *Discipleship*, ed. Geffrey B. Kelly and John D. Godsey, trans. Barbara Green and Reinhard Krauss (Minneapolis: Fortress Press, 2001), esp. 57–83.

13. Ibid., 59.

14. Ibid., 62.

15. Calvin, *Institutes*, 2:851.

CHAPTER 4: WITH WHOM DO WE PRAY?

1. This is widely assumed in North America and Europe, but perhaps less so in other parts of the world, and it is widely practiced among mainline Protestants and Roman Catholics, but perhaps less so by other traditions.

2. See, for example, Rom. 12:4–5; 1 Cor. 12:12–27.

3. See, for example, Acts 9:2; 18:25; 19:9, 23; 22:4; 24:14, 22.

4. Actually, Pauline authorship of Colossians is highly disputed. Many scholars think it likely that the letter was written by one of Paul's followers after his death. Nevertheless, because Paul is traditionally associated with this letter, we will use "Paul" as opposed to "the author of Colossians."

5. In using the terms "corporate" and "interpersonal," I have in mind the kind of prayer that takes place in more formal settings, like worship or prayer services, and also in informal set-

tings, such as when two or more people are gathered beside a hospital bed, at a Bible study, or around the dinner table, or when family members are getting ready for bedtime.

6. Here I draw on Donald Capps's discussion of "intentional" and "attentional" qualities of listening in *Giving Counsel: A Minister's Guidebook* (St. Louis: Chalice Press, 2001), 14; and on Deborah van Deusen Hunsinger's discussion of listening in *Pray Without Ceasing: Revitalizing Pastoral Care* (Grand Rapids: Wm. B. Eerdmans Publishing Co., 2006), esp. 28–98.

7. I have been influenced here by several thinkers, especially Karl Barth, Dietrich Bonhoeffer, Hans Frei, George Lindbeck, William C. Placher, and Gerard Loughlin.

8. Allan Hugh Cole Jr., *Be Not Anxious: Pastoral Care of Disquieted Souls* (Grand Rapids: Wm. B. Eerdmans Publishing Co., 2008), 172.

9. See, for example, Rom. 12:12; 2 Cor. 3:18; Phil. 3:20–21.

10. The hymn is often titled "Blessed Assurance, Jesus is Mine." Unfortunately, this connotes possessing Jesus, which too much of contemporary Christianity lauds. Nevertheless, the hymn as a whole conveys that we belong to Jesus and that we do so as we share his story.

11. See, for example, 1 Cor. 13:13; Gal. 5:5–6; Col. 1:4–5; 1 Thess. 1:3; 5:8.

12. See also, for example, 2 Cor. 1:11; 1 Thess. 5:25; 2 Thess. 3:1; Phlm. 1:22.

13. For a fuller treatment of this claim, see Allan Hugh Cole Jr., *Good Mourning: Getting through Your Grief* (Louisville, KY: Westminster John Knox Press, 2008), esp. 71–92; and Cole, *Be Not Anxious*, esp. 192–214.

14. See, for example, Matt. 14:23; 26:36; Mark 6:46; 14:32; Luke 5:16; 9:28.

CHAPTER 5: HOW DO WE PRAY?

1. See also Allan Hugh Cole Jr., *Good Mourning: Getting through Your Grief* (Louisville, KY: Westminster John Knox Press, 2008), 86–87.

2. John Calvin, *Institutes of the Christian Religion*, 2 vols., ed. John T. McNeill, trans. Ford Lewis Battles (Philadelphia: Westminster Press, 1960), 2:897.

3. Dietrich Bonhoeffer, *Dietrich Bonhoeffer Works*, vol. 5, *Life Together/Prayerbook of the Bible*, ed. Geffrey B. Kelly, trans. Daniel W. Bloesch and James H. Burtness (1999; repr., Minneapolis: Fortress Press, 2005), 157.

4. John Calvin, *On Prayer: Conversations with God*, intro. by John Hesselink (Louisville, KY: Westminster John Knox Press, 2006), 113.

5. See, for example, 2 Sam. 22:4; Ps. 17:6; 18:3; 55:16; 141:1; Isa. 55:6; Jer. 29:12.

6. This approach is adapted from Deborah van Deusen Hunsinger's approach to memorizing Scripture. See *Pray Without Ceasing: Revitalizing Pastoral Care* (Grand Rapids: Wm. B. Eerdmans Publishing Co., 2006), 203.

7. Bonhoeffer, *Life Together*, 53.

8. Ibid., 162.

9. Ibid., 54–55.

10. Hunsinger, *Pray Without Ceasing*, 36.

11. For a fuller treatment of this claim, see Allan Hugh Cole Jr., *Be Not Anxious: Pastoral Care of Disquieted Souls* (Grand Rapids: Wm. B. Eerdmans Publishing Co., 2008), 192–214.

12. Hunsinger, *Pray Without Ceasing*, 37.

13. Frederick C. Mish, ed., *Webster's Ninth New Collegiate Dictionary* (Springfield, MA: Merriam-Webster, Inc., 1988), 83.

14. See Cole, *Good Mourning*, 87–89.

15. See Thomas Keating, *Open Mind, Open Heart: The Contemplative Dimension of the Gospel* (1986; repr., Minneapolis: Fortress Press, 1993).

CHAPTER 6: HOW DO WE KEEP PRAYING?

1. Dietrich Bonhoeffer, *Dietrich Bonhoeffer Works*, vol. 5, *Life Together/Prayerbook of the Bible*, ed. Geffrey B. Kelly, trans. Daniel W. Bloesch and James H. Burtness (1999; repr., Minneapolis: Fortress Press, 2005), 156, emphasis added. See Luke 11:1–13 and these additional examples of Jesus giving instruction in prayer: Matt. 6:9 13; 7:7–11.

2. For a fuller discussion of the role of life patterns and habits, see Allan Hugh Cole Jr., *Be Not Anxious: Pastoral Care of Disquieted Souls* (Grand Rapids: Wm. B. Eerdmans Publishing Co., 2008), 188–91.

3. William James, *Talks to Teachers on Psychology; and to Students on Some of Life's Ideals* (New York: Literary Classics of the United States, 1987), 750.